THE OPTIONAL SOCIETY

THE OPTIONAL SOCIETY

AN ESSAY ON
ECONOMIC CHOICE AND BARGAINS OF
COMMUNICATION IN AN AFFLUENT WORLD

by

FOLKE DOVRING AND KARIN DOVRING

MARTINUS NIJHOFF / THE HAGUE / 1971

ISBN 90 247 1278 5

PRINTED IN THE NETHERLANDS

To CASSANDRA

PREFACE

Long before today's electronic media made us aware of articulate "world opinions" across the globe, there were other dramatic international communications. One current of opinion was expressed by the many generations of different nationalities who "voted with their feet" and settled down in North America. To them and to many others, the hallmark of the United States since the beginning of the republic was the freedom of choice for common people. This image was inspiring enough to build up the free institutions which together with the country's open frontiers broke the hold of mass poverty. So, options brought to the masses are America's trademark in human civilization.

Nowadays, when advanced industrialization and electronic media are penetrating the world and opening new frontiers everywhere, the challenge from the optional society – often called "Americanization" – becomes a source of global competition, imitation or opposition and shapes the profile of our time.

What is the character of this new optional society so early displayed in the United States but today emerging in many other countries and communicated wherever nations confront socio-economic problems of their own? Can analysis of its economics and communications reveal its international message? More than two decades of research in those fields and our experience as Americans by choice have made us try.

It is by no coincidence that the continuous expansion of options at home and abroad is felt as a time of crisis in the United States. Open the window and you feel the wind. Opportunities create problems, but for each problem there are opportunities too. It is hardly news to say that our society is sick; all dynamic societies are, in one way or another. But as with individuals, societies' ailments say something about their deepest character. Forecasts for the future are of no use, and one-sided vilification is no better than mindless glorification. Rather, we need to know ourselves. We need to reflect on the meaning of our expanding options. How we use them or not use them may decide whether they will be destroyed or still be open in times to come.

Urbana, Illinois, U.S.A., June 1971.
Folke Dovring   Karin Dovring

TABLE OF CONTENTS

CHAPTER I

THE KEY WORD IS CHOICE

It may come as a surprise to many: one of the most basic facts of modern life is the widening range of choice. Wealth makes free, but it liberates the most when it is shared by many. Our modern affluent society, so often berated for its materialism and mass "consumerism," actually leaves people more free choices than any other society in the past or in the contemporary world. It even leaves us the option to do away with poverty which so long has been the multitude's choiceless fate.

There is so much else to attract our attention today that the fact of freedom to choose is often overlooked. Many people miss the choices by making up their minds in advance. Many others feel oppressed by the many decisions they have to take – from cigarette brands to politics – that this too leads them to underrate, or to take for granted, the freedoms we actually have. Fears and perils are not typical for our time only, nor are prophets, rebels or rabblerousers. Marcuse is no more a novelty than Billy Graham, and our latterday revolutionaries are mere imitators. It is commonplace today to claim that no age has had troubles like ours. All ages agree. No age has had worse troubles than its own!

The freedom to choose is not new altogether, but new to our time is the expansion of choice. Not only is there more to choose from; there are also many more people who have (or could have) a choice. As individuals: never before did the many have any real leeway. As societies: at no time before could whole communities take stock of their situation and decide what direction to opt for. As a case in point think of the "women's liberation movement": the civic and human equality of the sexes has really not been materially possible much before our time. This liberation conjures up a vast array of options in visions and meanings.

The fact is that we are heading for – and to some handsome extent already are in – an optional society, one where people may come a long way toward choosing the kind of life they will live. *May*, because they are not certain to exercise their options. *Choose,* because even not exercising the options is in itself a choice, like it or not.

This expansion of choice comes from material affluence and grows with it. Here is where the great paradox comes in: by raising our material level of living, modern technology, economics, and communication also give us the means to live less under their spell. We have the option to devote more of ourselves to pursuits which are closer to our hearts than to our pocket books. It is not as the Marxians say that food and shelter came *before* cultural pursuits; these were all to some extent there from the start of mankind. But shortage of material necessities dictated many constraints on what the cultural pursuits might be. They defined, for instance, women's role in society. The fate of "Shakespeare's sister" (Virginia Woolf) is a dramatized instance of the waste of human talent in a society of penury. But most of this waste is not on record and therefore we cannot see it.

One of the standing complaints against modern society is its materialism, or its predominant interest in tangible things, in contrast to affairs of the soul such as art, moral, and religion. Such excessive preoccupation with material goods is very likely a passing stage in the transition from penury to affluence. This materialism has also been exaggerated in the minds of many moral critics. The overwhelming fact is of course that only with material affluence can we be free in our choices. And this goes both for the art, moral and religion, and for the politics and society of our choice.

Those who credit the societies of traditional poverty with a more spiritual outlook do not know enough history. Therefore they do not have enough perspective on the modern affluent society they are browbeating either. Traditional society may appear to have been more devoted to art, moral, and religion than one discovers at a first glance in modern industrial communities. But to the extent this was or is true – in part it is an optical illusion of hindsight – it was from necessity, not choice. When there are few material goods to go around, and less still of a chance to increase their supply, more time may be left for cultural pursuits – except when the whole society was laid waste by hunger, sickness, and warfare, as happened too frequently. Options were at best a privilege of the very few at the top of society – nobility, mandarins, and commissars, for instance – those who drew their wealth from the sweat of the masses. But even the privileged few were often hampered in exercising their options (as they may have seen them) by the risk of offending the poverty-trained emotions and mores of the masses. Renaissance Popes who were irreligious art lovers offended the believers and sparked Reformation, eventually also a counter-reformation to enforce more austerity on the Catholic Church itself. Lavrenti Beria, Stalin's last henchman, might have survived his master longer had he not so blatantly violated public Communist ethics in his own private debaucheries.

Slavery enslaves the master too, and the upper classes usually sustained many kinds of censorship designed to maintain balance and stability in a social fabric dominated by mass penury. For the common man, lifelong poverty gave little choice but to worship the gods, follow the mores, and cultivate the arts which their community would approve of and could afford; and of course to obey its laws and institutions as if they were God-given inevitabilities. Material necessity defined the scope for growth of the spirit, more narrowly and more compellingly than in any materialistic modern society.

Human communication was also narrowly defined: in traditional societies, contact with other cultures was scanty and mainly hostile since the unknown or little known was felt as a threat to one's own identity and values. The local communication realm – the ghetto formed by the like-minded when they communicate their own society's ideas – was seldom influenced by foreign ideas. This left the common person with little to communicate other than the culture of his own narrow community.

Modern technology and the development of global mass media have in many ways broken up this parochial isolation. They have also caused enthusiastic reports of a "global village" where we are one people – mankind turned into one close family because of the technological get-together. This could be a dream or a nightmare depending on our viewpoint on what mankind should be. But as yet, the modern technological mass media merely link us together across the globe. They do not unite us. The expansion of options – the revolution of rising expectations, the meeting of global slum and global affluence – makes international communication a weapon of war as often as a means to peace. It is not unusual that the man on the global street turns all the more parochial the more cultural options he faces. For instance, the ethnic conflict of French Canadians has only been intensified by modern media.

Modern affluence and the expansion of our options that goes with it are not only new. They have also come upon us rather suddenly through one of the "threshold effects of history" – a gradual difference becoming absolute, as when the thermometer rises above the boiling point. The intellectual and technical sources on which modern affluence draws have been long in the making. They have been under way since the conquest of fire.

It is now evident that their coming has been continuously accelerating from an extremely slow start very long ago toward the more and more quickening pace which we are now witnessing. The threshold effect of modern industrialism came about because this industrialism made it possible, as it has never been before, to make production of life's necessities grow faster than the human population. It also gave us the means and the attitude for slowing down the growth of population which of course quickened the passing of the threshold in the countries where it happened that way. Even this threshold effect was not too obvious all at once, for the depth of mass poverty was such that it took time to accumulate enough wealth to make the broad public affluent.

But there are we now: in North America, Europe, Oceania, Japan, and piecemeal elsewhere, poverty is a minority feature. And that has never happened before. Along with the rising level of wealth and income, the incomes also tend to become less unevenly distributed among people in the affluent countries. The continuing plight of the masses in the "third world" countries is all the more dramatized by the comparison.

The society of expanding options is a show of promises and pitfalls. Less than ever would there be a place for a definite program of what society should be – let alone prophecies or forecasts of what it will be. The point here is what society might be at its richest – assuming that human freedom and dignity and variety of life have something to do with it.

In exploring this, economics and communication analysis are logical partners. Economics, taken in the wide sense, applies to all situations of choice and to how conflicting choices are brought in line with our accepted values. All human affairs have some economizing or "housekeeping" aspect: a case in point is the amount of time we afford ourselves to spend in front of our television screen.

Communication analysis helps us understand our own values and other communities'. How the values are communicated – built up, maintained, changed, or destroyed to make room for new options. The communication of ideas first establishes the ground rules along which our choices are made. At the same time, this communication depends on choices which in many situations also are a case of economics. Everything said or done is at the cost of something else. Spot commercials on radio or television are not the only ones that count the minutes. Economists usually neglect the whole process referred to here and the formation of ideas which underlies the economic demand and supply which they discuss.

The engine of progress is the rising productivity which leads to affluence in goods and abundance of access to communication. The quest for luxuries is a key part of the process, for without luxury, most of the progress would not have come about. The rise in productivity has been and still is accelerating. The causes of this acceleration are both in the human mind and in the nature of its inventions. Affluence and acceleration are prodded along by competition. Contrary to what we are often told, competition is not vanishing; it is on the increase.

When we say progress, we usually mean that things are getting better. But are they? The meaning of poverty and wealth must be seen not only in what we have access to but also from what we really get. Let us ask in general: Do we get more satisfaction from the larger supply of goods and services? If so, how much of our increased satisfaction stems from greater security and how much from greater freedom – wider choice?

Now, satisfaction is hard to measure, and harder still is it to measure it over time – say, from one generation to the next. In the words of W. Arthur Lewis, what separates men from beasts is not happiness but freedom – the ability to do something about one's environment. Very likely, people of past centuries may have felt happier than we do, for in each slow-moving age they had more time to adjust to the limitations of their technology and society. Happier, that is, except for overwhelming fear of the unknown or when disaster really struck, and that occurred very frequently. The lower level of technology left less recourse for human ingenuity to take counter measures; so there was little security other than to accept "God's will."

If we sit down and count what we have, and what people had before us, there can be no reasonable doubt that much more satisfaction *is at our command* than was true of any generation before us. That is, if we use the opportunities.

This is in part a question of adjusting to new realities before they, too, become obsolete. Change is now so rapid that we are faced with the need to adjust to continuous change. Many people have great difficulty following the accelerating pace. People are biological beings; our internal rhythms do not permit unlimited acceleration in anything that concerns us directly. Often we are like a fly in the airplane happily flying around on her own encased in a monster of jet aviation. As consumers we grab for the fruits of technology changing from year to year in factories and laboratories. But when the human consequences come home to us by making many skills and occupations obsolete, this will strain many people and break quite a few. The "ordeal of change" (Eric Hoffer) is visited upon this generation more than upon any other generation. No more than this is needed to explain the turbulence of modern youth, searching for meaning and basic values.

That is why the expansion of options is accompanied by increasing uncertainty about the future. The question is why this should have to mean discomfort. Human nature was made for choice. The general reluctance to accept uncertainty is a hangover from past ages of penury. In those times, change would often threaten the whole material existence of many individuals. In the age of social security, the uncertainty of change still for many people threatens their place in the fabric of society.

It would be easy to believe that the uncertainty and even rootlessness in our affluent society would be balanced by our use of modern communication media. Never before have so many people been offered so many fast and inexpensive channels to contact their fellow men at home and across the globe. Long-distance calls – we are told – are the next best thing to being there; that is if we really want to be there! Loneliness may be a common plight in the affluent society, but despite this we often refuse to reach out to the stranger on Main Street even in the Global Village. And the most usual sign of contact, the dialog, is missing more often than not. Extreme examples are the military wives abroad who "just can't learn" the new language of their host country. And we can blame ourselves because the question is whether we really want to use our modern options to communicate. The uncertainty we feel through the rapid changes in our time is not likely to disappear through the more intensive contact that today's communication media offer. On the contrary, if we really want to use them and the options they give, we risk to face even greater uncertainty and even more unknown situations. People who dare out, or are forced out, of their parochial security to communicate with those who are different, will face even wider options when they try to get across in their message. Many times the responses they get will be quite unexpected or even incomprehensible.

The key word of it all is choice, and the human mental apparatus was made for choice. Basically we have got what it takes to use the breathtaking new opportunities for free selection. The neurons of our brain, numbering some one hundred thousand million, make it possible for us to handle unspeakable amounts of information and to reach astronomic numbers of variant conclusions, attitudes, and combinations of data. For the first time we may be able to use in full this brain capacity which has existed since a million years.

There are several question marks as to how an optional society will really function. How many people will refuse to accept the strain of change and choice? Many do this, in part or altogether, by addiction, by "dropping out" toward more primitive ways of life, or by shirking much of the burden through "non-involvement." How much of the newly-won freedoms will they destroy – for others and not just for themselves?

Complex as all this is, some of it will become more clear by analysis of the increasingly intensive interplay between economic factors and the communication of ideas. Communication is much more than transmittal of information. To make our options real, we need more than just a catalog of the great variety store that is our modern world. The goods must also be "sold" to us – that is, they must be presented in social terms which allow us to decide the consequences of our preferences. The usefulness, thrill, or prestige of all the many things at our reach must be linked with the values we cherish or reject.

This power of communication over economic processes explains why freedom to communicate is vital to all human freedom. Power over the communication process equals power, *tout court*. Without power of communication there can be no power over anyone, not even over oneself. Dictatorships typically claim monopoly not merely over the systems of transmission but also over the media's contents. The more extreme dictatorships even find ways to muffle private dissent between individuals. That this is easier done in the collectivism of a "People's Republic" shows how essential privacy is for freedom. The most vital distinction between free societies and tyrannies is not in the electoral system but in the freedom to communicate which alone can overcome the constraints of a political system.

The famous phrase that "In the present there is nothing but the past" (Bergson) always was an exaggeration. There is something new in every historical situation, and in our time of accelerating change more than ever before. The real impact of the new we shall miss, however, if we think that we are new altogether. Rebels programmed to be "historyless" risk to be captives of the past, and to repeat its mistakes, the more often the less they know about those old mistakes. Nothing could destroy the expansion of options more completely than an unthinking belief that our choices are completely free from our past. Freedom is always relative; only tyranny pretends to be absolute.

CHAPTER II

PRODUCTIVITY, LUXURY, AND POVERTY

Material progress comes from higher productivity. It is perhaps a paradox that many of the greatest strides toward higher productivity have been made in the production of necessities, and the most fascinating result of this is our greater access to luxuries. Let us first take a look at productivity and how it has risen, especially in our time. The acceleration of productivity is widely noted but little understood. The role of luxury for human progress has often been noticed, but its meaning for our expanding options has been neglected. Then there are problems of concept here: we can not talk about human progress without making clear the character of poverty.

Productivity

Our ability to produce more out of the same amount of human effort requires first of all that we improve technology. By technology we mean specialized skills and applied scientific insights. Even though this is necessary, it is not sufficient to make productivity increase. The nature of the social order is also very important here. There is more than one way to organize production. But there are also ways in which it can not be organized and still create affluence. For instance, factories in Japan are organized differently from those in the United States, but they are equally successful. One can not say the same of the collective farms in the Soviet Union which remain low productive despite huge amounts of machinery.

The social order in the wide sense also helps or hampers by inspiring attitudes to work, learning, and acquisition of skills – including the skills of organization. Classical economic theory talks about three groups of "factors of production:" Land, Labor, and Capital. To this can now be added the quality of labor and management.

The social order also sets the terms for communication. It decides, among other things, whether insights and skills will be widely diffused or confined to the specialists or maybe silenced altogether. Evolution could not be taught in American schools until the hold of Bible fanatics had been broken. Modern genetics could not be taught or practiced in the Soviet Union until the fanatics of "dialectical materialism" had brought the country's agriculture close to disaster by the doctrines of Lysenko and his followers. The social order even decides if there will be any market or not for some kinds of skill: here the under-rating of the salesman in the Soviet system contrasts against his prominent place in the United States.

Productivity is a word of several meanings, the technical ins and outs of which we shall not elaborate upon here. Instead we use it in its simplest and least technical meaning – a meaning which relates to the proportion between the amount of time and effort that is spent on production and the amount of goods and services produced. Rising productivity means, in those simple terms, that we get more for our time and effort.

It is necessary to keep apart the fact of rising productivity and its causes. If we produce more, the ultimate cause must be that we have become more "productive." People in the affluent society not only have more machines and other technical means to help in production. They have also more ability to replace them if they are destroyed; dramatic examples are the re-building of the war-damaged economies in countries such as Germany and Japan. In striking contrast, progress was much slower in countries which were poor and under-developed at the beginning of the post-war era. With advancing technology, people themselves are becoming different as producers. When some economists say that we are worth as much as we produce, this is self-evident but does not explain anything. The explanations lie in complicated technical, sociological, psychological and cultural changes. There is no merit in trying to reason away the fact that we on the whole get more for our time and effort today than did those who were before us.

There are some who try to belittle the increasing affluence by pointing out the many ambiguities in measuring income. Especially when it comes to the United States in recent decades, it has been said that the data on National Product are "increasingly meaningless." Such opinions reflect two things: one is the genuine difficulty of measurement, and the other is a condescending criticism of consumers' preferences.

The yardstick of all economic measurements reflects the values a society prefers. So if someone insists that his own value judgments are better than the general public's, he can of course criticize to his heart's delight in the belief that "I am holier than thou." To say that in the opulent society the general public has bad taste and does not know how to spend its money, is to underrate the common man. It is not only the mass media who use this argument as an excuse for their programs. One also hears the same opinion among economists who believe that the common man's taste is all a matter of commercial manipulation. Politicians know better: in a free society there are limits to the credibility gaps the public will tolerate. Not even in the Soviet Union do the authorities succeed in imposing their value standards. The general public reacts by extensive black market trading.

Difficulties in measurement of National Product are more serious, but this argument works both ways. It is true that conventional accounting in some ways tends to exaggerate the growth in income. Old-style handicraft production was not accounted for as long as it was not intended for the market, while the factory products which replaced it are included. Thus, especially in some early phases of economic development, the growth of national product incorporates an element of rising commercialization. It is true too that specialization brings with it many indirect costs which have not been estimated. The tiresome and costly commuting between home and place of work should be counted as a part of cost of production – it is hardly a part of leisure. The great convenience of access to many specialized products is also to some extent offset by the need for frequent shopping and substantial savvy on the quality and use of the goods. Many modern appliances may save us time and effort from home crafts and do-it-yourself projects. But often we make it into a dubious achievement; the housekeeper who devotes her excess time to playing bridge is not necessarily an exponent of progress.

Some of these hidden costs are a matter of what people do with the opportunities they have, as when increased leisure time is wasted. Others, as commuting for instance, could be incorporated in the national accounts by refined bookkeeping. Only recently has refuse disposal been generally understood as a hidden cost of very large proportions. Throughout all the hubbub on environment pollution, one major fact comes out: that we have enjoyed many good things of life without paying their full price. Re-cycling of materials that can be used again (such as metals and bottles), and destruction to innocent waste of those that cannot, will cost sizeable amounts. Ultimately this will be paid by consumers, no matter how the financing is engineered. Substantial as these costs are, they are not all that big. They mean – like the costs of commuting etcetera – that the amount of progress was in some degree smaller than we thought. But the essential of modern progress will still be with us when these costs have been accounted for, as they will be.

Hidden costs are not the only difficulty in measuring National Product. There is also hidden progress which is easily forgotten because it is taken for granted. For instance, when they ceased sending air mail letters by carrier pigeons and began using airplanes instead, the costs of the old system were soon forgotten. How many pigeons would be needed, and what would it cost to raise and use them, to send the present mass of air mail by such live carriers? No comparison is ever made with the much lower costs of plane service. The contribution of aviation is measured by its industrial costs, not by what it replaces. National accounts do not measure the productivity of a modern electronic computer by figuring out how many clerks would be required to replace it. Much of the work done by modern gadgets could not at all be done before. Carrier pigeons were not sent from New York to San Francisco or across the oceans, and huge numbers of clerks were never put to a computer's task of solving vast numbers of highly complex equations.

Such advances in *production* are overlooked partly because of the difficulties of measuring them, for reasons which are both conceptual and practical. Besides that, we get used to the novelties and cease to imagine how to do without them. Then it is a different matter that when once expensive services become cheap, they will be used for cheap purposes too. Air mail now carries a great deal of trivial and frivolous messages, and electronic computers are frequently asked to solve silly problems. But this *consumption* is a matter of how new options are used; it cannot belittle the technical achievements themselves.

There are ways in which we can show how real some of the achievements are. First we can find out the labor time spent in producing an essential commodity such as milk, for instance. Then we can compare this with the labor time a consumer needs to work to earn the wages to buy the milk. Both of these labor times, the producer's and the consumer's, have declined continuously and most sharply in recent time. Bread, steel, cloth, house heat and other things considered essential for our daily life can now be had for money which represents the wages for a few hours' work. Previously the same quantities would require days or weeks of toil. Such a measure of progress cannot be reasoned away.

Productivity gains have been very large in agriculture and manufacturing. But there is hardly any field where they have been so obvious as in the expansion of mass media. It is everybody's daily experience how much faster, cheaper and easier it is today to transmit messages than only a few years ago. The media's industry has however a venerable past. It began with the printing press in the fifteenth century which was the first real mass goods industry – and this first mass goods industry served communication. When tools and shoes were still made by hand, one by one, books became mass produced in hundreds and thousands of identical copies. It is true that some highbrow intellectuals at that time looked down their noses on the printing press and refused to read a printed book and stuck to the hand-made manuscript. Just as there were, not long ago, latter-day intellectuals of similar breed who refused to look at a television screen, let alone buy a set. But this reluctance to accept the tools for communication as a mass industry could not delay the increasing productivity of the mass media. The transmission of messages by telephone, telegraph and global satellites, or whatever the latest development happens to be, has been and is still accelerating.

When intellectuals many centuries apart gave a similar negative reaction to communication as a mass industry, then this points to another interesting fact. People's ability to communicate has not kept pace with the technical expansion and productivity of mass media. In some quarters the skill to communicate may even have declined. The modern media tend to talk to everybody but only listen to samples of their audience. Therefore they speak on our behalf but they do not communicate *with* us as a mass public. Eloquent people nowadays are no more eloquent than in the time of Homeros. The man in the street in London or Chicago may be even less articulate than in the past. The one-way television screen gives him an effortless involvement in life during peak hours or fringe programs but makes the majority of us silent.

Large as are the gains in technical productivity, much of them could be whittled away if the labor force were not to keep up its quality. The deterioration of many services in the United States such as the telephone service in New York is a warning that a high standard of living cannot be maintained automatically just because high-level technology is employed. The people operating the system must remain on the level of accuracy no less than knowledge which the technology requires. Or else the whole modern prosperity might go down the drain for lack of maintenance.

Our higher productivity does not mean that we are "better." Many would say that we are worse and this might be plausible. When we can get more for the same effort, the choice might be between that and the same for less effort. Most people will want a little of both – in short more for less effort. All told, it is quite possible that most modern people in the affluent countries exert themselves less in their work than did people in previous generations. And this might have some negative effects on our character. Again, it is hard to tell, for we are in the thick of our own problems and might easily idealize a past which is no longer present. The side chores of commuting and shopping add more strain to our days. The increased strains of adjusting to accelerating change may also tax us as heavily as once did long hours of painstaking manual work.

Acceleration

Acceleration of technical change in our days is generally known and widely noted. It is in fact not even a new trend: it has been going on since many centuries – ever since the conquest of fire. Before the Industrial Revolution, the acceleration of progress was generally overlooked because it was overshadowed by shorter or longer episodes of success or disaster. The principal evidence for this many centuries' long acceleration of technical progress is in the growth of human population which has been slower, the farther back in time we go. This multi-secular population trend reflects the rising ability to provide for more people. People's ability to multiply has always been far ahead of technology. When we say that technology sets the upper limit for the size of a surviving population, we must take the concept of technology in a very wide sense indeed. It then includes the social order and all its supporting factors in church discipline, military system, and civil administration. All of this had to be invented and tested out over long periods, no less than was the case with the ploughs and the swords.

Until the last century or two, technical progress was more in the arts than through science. Inventors were usually innocent of the science of their days. Johannes Kepler, the seventeenth century astronomer, once sat down to calculate the ideal form of a wine keg, using the newest mathematics of the day. No sooner had he solved the problem than he found that illiterate craftsmen since long were making the kegs as his formulas suggested. Such practical inventions were made on intuition. Even so, many inventors unwittingly drew on common-sense knowledge which had once been a feat of advanced science, such as the art of writing, arithmetic, geometry, or sailing by compass. For older periods, we can not clearly keep apart the role played by science and the contributions from unconscious groping in the practical arts. We should not underrate the role of intuition in our days either. Pre-scientific achievements gradually built up a body of knowledge which made possible a more and more systematic approach to the problems of mastering nature. The habit of handling elementary mechanical gadgets such as wheels, blocks and sliding planes must have prepared the human mind for science and advanced technology by the schooling in rational thought which such gadgets provided. The many centuries' long acceleration of progress can be explained by the gradual "tooling up of the mind." Such an explanation also fits the modern phase with its systematic application of science to technology. Many tools of the advanced science of the past have become common-place machines to which technicians and students get accustomed at an early age: many young people now are as familiar with an automobile motor as their grandfathers were with horses.

The accelerating trend is now quite obvious and the tempo still appears to be rising, among other things because larger and larger parts of the world are directly participating in scientific research and technological experimentation. Major breakthroughs in science now tend to be of larger and larger consequence because science becomes more basic, permitting a more generalized grip on reality and larger practical leverage for better or worse. Atomic power took much shorter time to develop from pure theory to applied uses than either steam power or electricity. Technical innovations are also more and more often "market induced," that is, made in response to recognized needs. The time lapse from basic invention to blueprint and from there to mass production also tends to become shorter and shorter. "Inventions are not made, they happen," someone said not long ago. The impression is, more and more, that if an invention is not made here and now, it soon will be made somewhere else.

This acceleration of technological progress has much with it that is good. It is really the reason for mass affluence. It is also why we can hope that mass affluence will become general the world over within the lifespan of today's children.

Acceleration also increases the strains on people who have to catch up and hang on in the rising tempo of change. There are two very unsettling types of problems that follow the tracks of accelerating progress: "second-generation problems" and the tragedies of obsolete skills and competence.

"Second-generation problems" are all those after-effects from new technology which could not be foreseen. Such after-effects on the physical environment are most easily dramatized, and sometimes overdone by the zealots of environment control. High yielding crop varieties often prov· vulnerable to pests and diseases, as happened in the corn blight of 1970. To keep up the progress such varieties represent, therefore requires continued biological research. Chemical means of controlling weeds, insects, and disease often upset the ecological balance of surrounding nature. Air and water pollution and scrap disposal are no new problems, but mass affluence has given them a new dimension in quantity. After-effects on the social and human environment are often more difficult to describe. Mechanization of agriculture and automation of factories often uproot large numbers of people – and what this means depends on how soon these people can find new employment and new stable social relations.

One of the great strains from acceleration has to do with our acquisition of knowledge and skills. Technological change becomes not only personally taxing but also causes economic hardship when many skills which people learn when they are young are bound to become obsolete within their lifetime. Nowadays it is not only many specialized skills that threaten to become obsolete, forcing the individual to retrain to be useful again. But sometimes the whole direction of study and work becomes so different that readjustment means loss of both status and income. Displaced farmers often join the ranks of the lowest paid and least regarded members of urban society. In the United States large numbers of black people were displaced when cotton growing was mechanized, and they found their field skills to be of no use in the cities. In Europe the opposite solution was adopted: surplus peasants were kept on the farms as long as possible because their underemployment there would be more acceptable than unemployment and social degradation in the cities. In the under-developed countries the displacement of peasants is even more irrational when the newcomers in the cities not only have no skills for which there is any market but do not find any drudgery jobs either. The skill of the individual small merchant also tends to go down the drain with business concentration. The reaction of French small-business people in the short-lived Poujade movement parallels earlier revolts by craftsmen against modern methods of production. In our days these things happen even faster, and many people never had any chance to anticipate what skills would become obsolete. The rash of "future research" which is spreading across the western world only underscores this, for among all its forecasts very few can be made with much confidence. The best that can be offered the young is a general readiness for the "future shocks" to come, but not many suggestions as to what these shocks will be.

Acceleration as such cannot go on forever. If it did, many of the changes would become absurd. It has been pointed out that in the domain of physics, continuous acceleration would cause a whole process to "burn out" at some stage – from overheating. The analogy is not complete in economic and social processes, but there are reasons why these processes cannot go on accelerating forever. Some braking factors are already at work. Many business firms are unwilling to invest in new gadgets every year, because the old ones would then have to be scrapped before they have served their useful lifetime and been depreciated to near zero. For instance, some airlines chose to pass up the turbo-prop generation of airplanes, because the jet planes were expected to come so soon after. Durable investments place a ceiling on the rate at which innovations may follow upon each other. But even with this "jumping of stages," some of the acceleration is still maintained.

Growth in per-capita national product may eventually be slowed down by its own built-in logic. When productivity rises rapidly in the making of some goods, we shall soon get as many of these goods as we want, and then expansion of them has to stop. For instance, this is at the root of agriculture's problems in modern America. But there are things where productivity can rise only slowly or not at all. Such things include live theatre and scarce natural beauty. A building lot overlooking a breathtaking lakefront "produces" aesthetic pleasure, but this "production" cannot be increased or made cheaper. The richer people get, the more the attractive lot will cost, its share in national product will increase. The same can not be said of mass produced inexpensive high-rise apartment buildings; the demand for them will be saturated.

Modern economic progress may at last turn out a society where mass production of essential goods requires only a small part of all our time and effort. Then we have the option to devote the rest to our individual interests and cultivate our personalities in the degree they can stand a spiritual civilization. A utopian dream? It is closer than you think. When society as a whole has arrived to such opulence, luxuries will be the intelligent escape hatch from the boredom of ever-growing heaps of mass goods.

Luxury

Across the ages, luxury has turned many wheels for progress. Benjamin Franklin was a naive economist, and his "Poor Richard" is for good reasons laughed at anew each time other naive amateurs discuss economics the way he did. On one point he hit something essential, however: when he talked about the beneficial effects of our quest for luxuries. How strong a motive this is we can see from plenty of historical cases. There is also a special logic to the greater dynamism in luxuries compared to the grubbing for sheer necessity.

Let us begin with the most archaic and backward tribes on the face of the earth. Natives of the interior highlands of New Guinea, one of the remotest, most untouched corners of the world, lived until quite recently in the Stone Age. Usually they trade a good deal with their close neighbors, who in turn trade with their neighbors, and so on, so that a vast trade network is spread over wide areas. The trade is mainly in luxuries, the goods are often frivolous such as birds' feathers and beads, used to adorn the body and create social prestige. The only necessity traded widely was salt, because it is not a product of these highlands. Axes are also traded, and recently steel knives made in distant factories have found their way into the circuit; useful as these are, the natives could live without them in their world of subsistence gardeners and hunters.

Now it has been shown that without the trade in luxuries not even the necessities would have reached all of these New Guinea people. Without birds' feathers and beads to go around, the people who supply the salt and the axes would at best have traded with each other if they at all had succeeded in finding each other. The ever-present luxuries created a coherent trade network on which the more scarce necessities, such as salt, could get a free ride. Without the luxury trade, salt would never have reached the highlands, and then it is doubtful that the highlands could have been settled at all; the natives' avidity for salt shows that they could not even exist without salt being brought into their area.

It is not enough to say that luxury often was an indispensable vehicle for trade. In ages of true penury, it was also the only sensible vehicle for trade. People could take risks on luxuries, because they could afford to lose them. People could not afford to risk being without food and other necessities. If the food could at all be physically produced at home or nearby, then it had to, even at very high cost. Primitive societies which might have tried to rely on distant supply sources would soon have perished in a famine. No country of any consequence has lived without its own food farming, and the density of population mirrored the country's capacity to produce food.

Transportation set the limits for trade in bulky goods. Grain and building materials are expensive to ship long distance. Through most of history, both ships and caravans had small capacity and even this at high cost and risk. The only things that could keep them moving were highly treasured goods. The Bible tells how King Solomon sent out a large expedition to the Land of Ophir to mine for gold and precious stones. The "Silk Road" across Asia brought Chinese embroideries to the Vikings' Europe. The quest for spices and precious metals sent Vasco da Gama and Christopher Columbus in their small ships across unexplored waters. Early America earned its way in contemporary Europe by selling tobacco – a new luxury in the Old World. Early French capitalism got its foreign money from exporting wine and luxury clothing and accessories. Japan's industri-alization was long based on exports of silk and toys.

Sending bread grain on shiploads after shiploads could be done under the Roman Empire because it dominated the entire Mediterranean as no other power has done. Bulk trade in grain was again started in late Mediaeval Europe. Supplies from the eastern Baltic lands were shipped to the maritime merchant cities in Germany, the Low Countries, and England. But it was a small part of all food which went that way, and the merchants in the cities still made much of their best money from luxury business. One of them, the great Fugger, is said to have made a fire of cinnamon bark to warm the chilled hands of Emperor Charles V. This may be a mere anecdote, but it is symptomatic of the then current image of the super-rich merchant: as one with large supplies of things which men can live without. Centuries later, farms in Belgium could prosper in proportion to the demand for their production of linen, much of which went to the new rich class in South America – then a supplier of European luxury consumption of sugar, coffee, and cocoa. As late as in the nineteenth century, Sweden spent as much money on importing coffee as she took in on exporting iron.

It is only in the last 100-150 years that non-luxury mass goods have dominated world trade. The coming of railroads and steamships, them-selves mass products of modern industry, first made this possible. Grain, coal, iron ore, oil in big tankers, and so on, these muscles of industry are now moving to where they are most in demand. No longer does a country have to be fed out of its own soil. No longer do the knives have to trail the birds' feathers. The options of supply sources extend to all corners of the world, as Japanese entrepreneurs are welcome in Alaska and the Pacific U.S.S.R., and their oil tankers ply the seven seas.

But the non-luxury character of modern world trade is in part an il-lusion. Such huge quantities of "essentials" could not be transported were it not for people's willingness to pay which reflects their quest for a higher standard of living. Much of the hardware that is traded goes into re-frigerators and television sets and sports-fishermen's equipment and lawn-mowers for well-to-do suburbanities. If we were all of a mind such as those American Indians who deplore "greed," to speak nothing of their self-styled modern followers among hippies and "flower children," then little else than preparation for war could keep on expanding the traffic of big ships and heavy rail cargo.

The lust for luxuries has been decried as greed, frivolity, vanity, lust for power and other character faults. Too much and too little spoils everything, and many vices are the exaggeration of a virtue or a harmless trait. No matter how we judge the moral aspect of luxury, we want to stress how indispensable luxury has been as a prime mover of progress. Luxury has started the trade which has caused much of the cultural contact without which we would all be stone-age hunters, if we existed at all.

It is therefore logical to suggest that many of the low-income countries in the tropics could take a leaf out of the book of early industrial Japan and go farther than they now do in cultivating the luxury instincts of the already affluent parts of the world. Art objects, handicraft goods, and tourism combined with local performing arts, all of this could amount to "exporting native culture" which really was the essence of the early Japanese trade story. True, the needs of the present low-income countries for foreign exchange is much larger than was Japan's in the decades around 1900 – but so are the mass markets for luxury goods and tourism in the affluent countries.

Luxury is far more than fancy goods and services. It is also communication. And communication of luxuries is two-faced, as we shall see on many points. The history of luxury communication is replete with both – the communication of luxuries and the communication as a luxury. Marxian theory would have us believe that bread and shelter come first and culture second. This is one of the Marxians' most basic errors. Culture comes at the same time as material essentials and always did. No one could make a loaf of bread – or eat it – without a substantial amount of culture. Eating taboos in India and elsewhere are not the only examples. World literature gives others, from almost any culture; let us only mention Hans Christian Andersen's tale about the girl who trod on the bread to save her shoes – a gross sin in the poverty-ridden ethics of Northern Europe.

In traditional societies, new crops spread slowly, as did the news about them. In matters of subsistence essentials, peasants always were distrustful as they had to be. Lighthearted trust would easily court disaster. In the game people played against nature for survival, risk minimizing dominated over profit maximizing. This trait could be modified only in large, organized and stable societies; examples are in the higher degree of progress in China and Japan, compared to India, in past centuries.

But news of heroes or rumors of fantastic events could move much faster and easier because here people's basic existence was usually not at stake any more than in the case of luxury objects. This kind of literary concern runs in unbroken line from the Homeric epics, through the Icelandic sagas and the "chevalier errant" novels in the century of Cervantes, all the way to modern television's weekly series on "wandering do-gooders" who have gun and will travel.

The ease by which literary luxury was spread in the old world explains a great many things in the history of communication. Characteristic is the way the printing press emerged in fifteenth century Europe. In the beginning it served above all the religious quarrels around the late Mediaeval Church. Thus it was society's mythological superstructure and *not* its material needs which called forth one of the most far-reaching innovations of all time. Lutheran Reformation could hardly have succeeded without the printed medium, and the option for common people to read the Bible spread literacy throughout the Lutheran countries. The "non-essential" (theology) spurred and accelerated change in the "essentials." Therefore the printed medium could be there to spread new agricultural technology when economic change began to make this possible.

Luxury played the same role of prime mover when it comes to advertising. Its "shocking history" has been replete with extravagant claims for dubious merchandise such as patent medicine, and other things which a God-fearing yeoman could do without. This character of aggressive advertising stems from the very nature of the merchandise. Because the goods were dubious, they could only be moved by "hard sell." The selling of the frivolous and the fraudulent became a testing of wits, both of sellers and buyers.

A small-town newspaper in southern Sweden for many years carried every day an obscure ad: "Buy Herman Svensson's well-liked bread." This uncommunicative ad was in fact a subsidy to the paper; it never sold any bread. The bread, widely known as "Sandby loaf" sold briskly to customers who never heard of Mr. Svensson. Good bread sells itself without advertising. Trade in grain or coal is also a matter of business correspondence and some bickering over price, but hardly of salesmanship. The buyer has already decided to buy and only shops around for supply source and price. By contrast, a tooth-paste with sex-appeal as its principal attraction will require hard selling indeed, for even the credulous will need much persuasion.

The patent medicines and other dubious frills have been the modern counterpart of Stone Age's birds' feathers: they have speeded up the pace of commerce and prepared the ground for cheaper production and wider distribution of essential goods. In the end, H. G. Wells' classical critique of capitalist society was overdone with the ingredient of hindsight: maybe uncle Teddy Ponderevo was not a total social parasite after all. His patent medicine Tono-Bungay, bunko as it may have been, did some good not merely because some customers thrived on what they believed (as in home-opathic medicine), but also because he intensified the competition for the public's money and made business grow. The patent medicines had effect not so much because of what they contained but more by the way they were communicated.

Economic production is not insensitive to that kind of impulses. The Nobel-Prize winning economist who recently confessed that he had just discovered that the stock market also had a "psychological" side, really displayed more naiveté than one expects from those quarters. People's optimism and pessimism is however much more than a psychological aspect of the stock market. Economic production will expand or contract in response to mental stimuli, and the patent medicines did their share. When business is slow, any kind of expansion is welcome by its "multiplier effect." Lord Keynes, advocating public-works programs for the unem-ployed, once retorted to his critics: "Let them (the unemployed) dig holes in the ground and fill them up again if they have nothing better to do – at least they will eat." Their wages, even from unproductive employment, would set business moving. So does optimism – and luxuries.

It is characteristic too that many of advertisement's detractors have accused the salesmen of "creating new needs" – as if that were not an essential part of any development toward higher living standards. In the long run, frugality is a poor vehicle of progress. The turn-of-century Kan-sas farmer who declared that "a house is a house, a meal is a meal, a dame is a dame, and that is all there is to it" would soon bring progress to a halt, were he the typical citizen over some prolonged period of time. So would thrifty suburbanites who think life is just having two cars in the garage and fighting the crabgrass in the backyard. Expansion of demand and its communication is vital to economic expansion, ultimately to improved human conditions.

Advisers to low-income countries these days know better than to limit the creation of new needs. Economic development requires, among other things, that demands are created – for bicycles and transistor radios or whatever can elicit increased effort. Such appeals will increase the supply of agricultural produce more than any technical instruction to peasants stooped in tradition.

Thus communication creates economic values, making real many options which would remain dormant without it. But apart from serving as a vehicle of economic progress, communication itself is in many cases a luxury in its own right. Advertisements may be strictly for business, but even they can contribute to our luxury by being entertaining, and under all circumstances they reflect the culture of their country. Sellers of French cheese and champagne glamorize their supplies by draping them in the *gloire* from Louis XIV to De Gaulle.

The role of communication for economic progress was often obscured in America where the quest for down-to-earth necessities out-shouted the sellers of culture. European paupers crossed the ocean and came to a fount of affluence far more abundant than anything within their reach in their old countries. Landless sons of landless farmhands became owners of rich prairie land large as a lesser manor in Europe. Assiduous toil would then make them rich by any of the standards they had grown up with. This could be done with essentially the same technical insights learned the hard way in Europe and with very little communication. What little communication there was tended to be overlooked because it was taken for granted. Dexterity, industry and thrift, trained and tooled up in the hard competitive school of European poverty both rural and urban were let loose on the rich virgin resources of America. In the process, some essential lessons were forgotten. Drawing on a technical and intellectual heritage from Europe which they had in their baggage, Americans for quite a while believed they could afford the coarse luxury of anti-intellectualism. Combining the excess knowledge from Europe with the excess land of America, rural Americans thought communication less essential to their success than hard and faithful work. They felt they already "knew all about it" so they did not care to listen. That is why even America, despite the manipulative trait of its culture, could underrate the input of the communicator because he was known mainly by the derogatory term of huckster.

It is a paradox that the same mistake was made in Europe; H. G. Wells is in large company. European socialism has always distrusted the salesman. Communist countries long underrated the need of communication for trade to be efficient. This is one of the main sources of the Communists' economic failures, before they recently began to resume precommunist practices on this point as on so many others. This is a double paradox, for in the political sphere, Communists are extremely communication conscious. Maybe they resented the salesman as a competitor of the political huckster dignified as propagandist?

The lacking sense for communication in rural America carried over into modern technological society. People marvelled at the new developments of technology in mass media. When a medium was new, its technology became a message, and for a while people could be fascinated just by listening to radio or watching color television. Some became fascinated enough to go for slogans such as the medium is the message, or to put it another way: the body is the spirit!

All new gadgets have an uncanny ability to grow old fast. The surprise wore off and our interest moved from the medium to the content of the program, and how many options it could offer. Preference for programs of pure entertainment among the public is evident if we trust the commercial sponsors who prefer a pleasant atmosphere in their customers' living rooms. The impressive amount of time which many people spend in front of their television sets is another sign of the scope of luxury in modern life.

Poverty

With all this opulence and luxury in the affluent society, there is poverty in our midst. Some poverty is obvious, but there are other kinds.

The attempt at launching a "war on poverty" provoked many gibes, some perceptive and many self-serving. Among other things we were offered the observation that many people, for instance in the backwoods of the Carolinas or among "Alabama hillbillies" had not been aware of being poor before and therefore were made worse off when it was pointed out that they were, indeed. The virtuous Alabama hillbilly had been a contented citizen, happy to let the cotton barons earn their bonanza on Federal farm subsidy and to keep the black people "in their place" and to vote for George Wallace. Now when they were officially declared poor, something new had been introduced in the picture, something that might upset the poor themselves and their politicians – not to mention the cotton barons. In a sense, then, the "war on poverty" made poverty more difficult for the poor to tolerate and more difficult for the rich to live with.

The "war on poverty" defined the poor as people living on less than so many specified dollars. Any such definition is arbitrary. Of course many things in society must be defined in arbitrary ways just to make administration function. But in a general discussion we can not dodge an issue on the same grounds that lawmakers and administrators have to. We need to define poverty. The puzzle is compounded when it appears that many poor in America have incomes on which people are well off in the abjectly poor countries. Do we merely have to adjust the currency exchange rates to get a more realistic picture, or do the realities of the modern industrial state pull jokes on our intellect? Is it not true that the poor in America often have access to things which would have been high luxury in past ages? So it goes, and those who decry the national-product data as increasingly meaningless get more grist for their mill.

International comparisons of levels of living are difficult indeed. Some physical needs, such as clothing, housing and house heating, vary with the climate. Moreover, the yardstick for measurement and comparison is the currency exchange rates which really measure only exchange relations of goods that are important in international trade. Those that are not, including housing and most services, can defy the exchange rates to almost any extent and mess up the whole comparison. Even between income levels in the same society comparisons may be difficult for partly the same reasons. Among other things, the rich and the poor may not buy their supplies in the same kinds of stores or use comparable qualities. In societies with sharp class distinctions it is not unusual to find that the rich are overcharged for the luxuries they buy. This is one way in which real income is re-distributed. At the other end of the scale, the poor are often cheated in the few stores where they can afford to buy. Poverty is expensive because of short planning horizon and few options for what and when to buy. The middle classes usually get their best money's worth out of what they spend because they have the economic leeway to use their options. They are seldom milked the way the improvident rich often are. The affluent society becomes optional, among other things, because it is dominated by the middle classes and their way of life.

None of this means that we have to give up on defining poverty or well-being. Levels of money income aside, there are actually some physical facts that give unambiguous clues.

The most obvious is in a decent level of food supply within the reach of the people concerned. The foodstuffs must be there and priced so that people can buy them with the incomes they have, allowing for their preferences between food and other things on which to spend money. This preference, as we shall see a little later, is relatively fixed at each level of income. But we still say available and within reach. The kind of malnutrition because of bad eating habits which is widespread in America among people who have incomes above the poverty line is a matter of neglecting the options they have. This is not really poverty in any accepted sense. But when bad eating habits are rooted in deep ignorance, they are undoubtedly a sign of poverty: the poverty of the culturally deprived. Such cultural poverty – on many income levels – is perhaps the most serious problem of the optional society. Undernourishment can be measured by objective tests. Often it is quite obvious as in some Asian countries where the common people are small and skinny while the well-to-do in the same country appear taller and more well-fed. Chronic undernourishment, especially in childhood, may impair the nervous systems and the mental abilities of a whole population. The transition from this to generally satisfactory, even though still Spartan, eating is one of the most consequential thresholds that a people can cross – the difference is far larger than measured by its money cost. Those who all their lives lived on the right side of this threshold can only with great difficulty imagine what this threshold means.

Another threshold is crossed when basic schooling becomes available to most if not all children and youngsters in a country – the schooling needed to be able to learn the skills of a modern economy. Again we must see the difference between available and being used. Some countries have had the material and financial means since some time but have missed the chance to education because of the egoism of the rich governing classes; there are examples in South America. In such a case the country is above that economic barrier but many of its citizens are not. On the other hand, there are countries, especially in Africa, which have striven so hard for basic literacy at an early stage of development that this distorts the use of their resources when there is no need yet for a mass mobilization of a modern labor force. The country is then still poor although it begins to give itself the appearance of having passed a threshold for which it is not yet ready. And again, if myopic school boards cause an adequately financed school system not to function because they meddle with the teaching of evolution, or insist on separate schools for ethnic and religious groups, then the community is not really poor but merely improvident in wasting the chances of its young.

A third threshold, which can be crossed only at a rather high level of per-capita income, is when essential medical service is available to all who need it. This threshold was crossed in Western Europe quite recently, and for economic and financial reasons it could not have happened much earlier. As a paradox, in the United States free medical service has not yet become a general reality. This is not due to the income level but to policy options which have had the upper hand so far. In a country such as the Soviet Union, the statistics may show very large numbers of doctors, nurses and dispensaries at work, but such data easily conceal the substandard quality of some of these services. They also conceal the fact that a large part of the country's rural population is far from having crossed this threshold – an achievement which would have required some redirection of national objectives away from sputniks and submarines.

Hard-core poverty in the United States takes on the character of a separate sub-culture: the "culture of poverty" (Oscar Lewis). Growing up in a ghetto of poverty also means belonging to a communication ghetto, a separate and narrow "communication realm." Because of its dependence on communication, poverty becomes its own cause and tends to perpetuate itself in its ghettos. In the midst of plenty, poverty depends on a poverty of the mind. In a wider sense, people are the poorer the fewer options they have and the richer, the wider the range of options which they have, know of, and are prepared to use. Many middle-class groups are poorer than they need be, because of self-inflicted limitations in an unimaginative and impoverished mental culture. In the United States, a good deal of this comes from the heritage of anti-intellectualism. The American university president who comes back from an official mission to India and blandly mentions that he could not understand the Indians' English, is in some ways a very poor man. Cultural poverty is the root of all other poverties, and the richer mind is the basis for an opulent society. Without a cultivated mind we cannot take full advantage of an affluent society's options.

CHAPTER III

COMPETITION IN THE MARKET PLACE

In the current folklore of economics, *competition* is vanishing. The advantage of bigness in most kinds of business is supposed to lead to more and more monopoly or at least to "oligopoly" where a few large firms divide the market between themselves. This easily leads to collusion between firms for price fixing which would pretty well eliminate the advantages which the consumers thought they once had under classical free competition. As if outright collusion were not enough, today's rapid means of transmitting information equally lead to implicit collusion. When all the firms have access to the same information about costs and prices, and at the same time, and all know a great deal about each others' business, they may set their prices as closely as if there were real collusion. In Middletown, U.S.A., where private firms compete for the homeowners' garbage disposal, the firms all charge the same basic fee, and they all come up with the same rate increases on the same dates.

Economics is not the only field to have its folklore. Some sociologists, and a good many psychologists, have wanted to downgrade the competitive way of life, or have tried to tell us that it is obsolete. The cooperative movement, for all its merits, has committed some excesses too. The slogan of "serving others" has been used to make a profit seem like a disservice.

Then there are, of course – even in capitalist societies – the public sectors, that is the government system. They are ever growing and using up a larger and larger part of the national product. And in the public sectors, there is no competition at all – everyone is supposed to know that for a fact. Only, when watching the infighting within bureaucracies one starts to doubt that fact.

This belief in the agony or near-death of competition comes, in a rather curious way, from one of the notions of standard economic theory, the so-called "theory of the firm." This theory assumes the business firm to be where economic decisions are made when it comes to production, pricing, and marketing. "Firms" here include also unincorporated small businesses, such as individual family farms for instance. The theory stemmed from the experience of the small industrial or trading firm of bygone days – a small concern, owned by a family or a close circle of investors. Before the "managerial revolution" even very large concerns could still be owned by a family and be run on lines resembling those of the classical small firm. The theory of the firm assumes the firm not to be at cross-purposes with itself and to be in effective competition with other firms.

Business concentration could eliminate competition when the small firms disappear. It is true that the small formally independent firm is still widespread in agriculture, some specialized crafts, and several lines of retail trade. But it no longer dominates either commodity production or the wholesale of most lines of retail trade, nor does it do so in banking and insurance. In most of today's economic life in an advanced country, firms are few and big and they are getting fewer and bigger by the year. That is why it is widely believed that business concentration is about to snuff out competition. As if to confirm the verdict, the last few years have seen the formation of huge "conglomerates" bringing together many kinds of business in a single giant firm. Even American anti-trust legislation is seen as rather without power to prevent the steady trend toward business concentration with all the dire consequences coming from this trend. In this "new industrial state," then, something else is needed to replace old-style competition. Or so the reasoning goes.

This "something else" is in fact already here, we contend. It is not so different from classical competition. It resembles it so much, in fact, that we intend to go on calling it – competition. The competition is not necessarily between firms in the same or similar business. Just as often it is between supply sources which may not appear to have anything in common at all. In the world of large corporations and conglomerates there is competition also within firms, as we shall see later. But first we must explain the very simple basis on which the new forms of competition rest: the increasing range of options, both in production and consumption.

These options take on several forms. First there are alternative raw materials out of which the same goods may be manufactured. Then there are options of different goods which may be used to serve the same final purpose. Further there are choices of what kinds of satisfactions the consumers want for their money when their rising affluence allows them to spend a growing part of their income as they please rather than just to meet sheer physical necessity. The options are also better advertised than ever before. Especially when it comes to alternative purposes of the consumers' spending, the rising pace and intensity of modern mass communication gradually make the choices more and more real for more and more people.

To these three categories, two more can be added: the competition within firms and bureaucracies, as already mentioned, and the options for employment and occupation.

In all five categories, it is important that one commodity or service may replace another one, either in production or consumption, what economic jargon calls "substitution."

Materials

If ever there was a risk of old-style monopoly, it was in the case of scarce raw materials. Oil trusts, for instance, tried to restrict the access to oil fields and to corner at least some part of the markets for petroleum products. Scarce metals such as copper and tin found in quantity only in a few countries could give much economic leverage to nations which happened to have these precious mines. In the imperial tradition of late nineteenth and early twentieth century industry, this economic power was taken over by international corporations which had concessions on these mines. More recently, the low-income countries in the tropics have hoped to improve their economic conditions by exploiting their collective monopoly on goods which only can be produced in their climate – rubber, hard fibers, coffee, spices, dyes, and numerous other materials. Wars have been fought over the access to tropical spices, continents were discovered and far-flung empires once built for these and similar reasons. As long as such scarce resources still were important, they were to a great extent owned and handled by the few colonial powers. In the nineteenth century, Latin America was the only tropical region where domestic elites had much direct control over their countries' resources, but these elites were just as egoistic in exploiting the masses of their own countries as any colonial administration, or worse.

The control over raw material sources was in fact a large part of the rationale for colonialism. The dismantling of the colonial empires is also symptomatic of the shift in the materials' markets that has taken place. The lessening of dependence upon specific raw materials which we see nowadays was anticipated by late nineteenth century German chemists who challenged German colonialism by claiming that their country would not need colonies. Chemical research laboratories and factories would produce artificial substitutes and make the scarce raw materials less coveted. Some early successes were spectacular and could be hard felt in a single country, as when Mexico's lucrative export of cochineal (a bright red dyestuff of insect origin) went down the drain, replaced by a far cheaper man-made chemical. Other early achievements were less glamorous but had larger impact at home, as for instance in the invention of "vegetabilic meat extract" and artificial flavors used in bouillon cubes from German cartels such as Liebig and I. G. Farben. Such exploits made the German word for substitute, *Ersatz,* a global by-word.

What the nineteenth century started is now happening on a grand scale and at an accelerating rate. Raw materials are getting increasingly versatile, capable of being transformed in more and more ways. Stuff derived from the same primary materials is made to serve more and more productive purposes. This large role of chemistry in modern life not only creates environment problems but also gives us the means of tackling them. This impact of chemistry is in itself a major part of modern productivity improvement. Basically everyone benefits; for some, the benefits are however so indirect that they do not notice them. Therefore, many believe that their business is only hurt by the chemical competition.

Out of wood, coal, and oil we get rubbers, fibers, plastics, and a vast and steadily multiplying array of chemicals for nearly as many technical and medical uses. This creativity of the chemical laboratories began on small proportions but is now snowballing. Since many years, synthetic rubber factories supply more rubber than all the tropical plantations taken together. Rayon, nylon, orlon, dacron, not to mention fibers made of milk or glass, have replaced natural fibers in many technical uses and give wool and cotton a good run on the markets for clothing. Plastics not merely serve a large number of essentially new technical purposes but also compete with glass and metals for many of their traditional uses such as containers and tubing. Cartons made of wood pulp are an equally successful alternative to glass and metalplate for many types of containers. And so on.

Almost as spectacular is the rate at which metals and other anorganic raw materials are being transformed so they can serve a wider array of purposes. Electric conductors are no longer always made of copper; aluminum can now be shaped and treated in ways that make it a good substitute. A still cheaper substitute, wires made from organic fibers, is said to be waiting in the wings. Aluminum also competes with steel for many of its traditional uses. Steel, for its part, is no longer a single material; alloys and other technical specializations of steel have rendered it extremely versatile, with numerous alternatives – of alloying, etc. – for obtaining the same technical service. Closer to the source, new methods of treating iron ore have made it profitable to obtain the raw stuff from many more alternative mine sites.

All of this increased substitution – technically and economically – means first of all increased competition: between industries, but also between countries and between regions within a country, and between the concerns and corporations which carry the interests of the various countries, regions, and industries. The chance to form a monopoly on any one material has been undercut by the increasing possibilities to substitute. Old-fashioned comparative advantage which relied upon the known natural resources of a country or a region – that advantage is now waning. New resources are being invented where none were thought of before, and some old resources are becoming obsolete or less profitable.

Another form of comparative advantage consists in the technological tradition of some industries in a country – the specific skills built up over long periods of competent and successful production. That kind of advantage is diminishing in value too. Technological progress is now so rapid that the advantage of a top-quality producer can be reversed by a decade of progress. This is how the watch making industry in the United States, recently fostered by tariff protection, has bypassed the old masters of Switzerland with the new technology of the tuningfork replacing the spring. This is also how Japan has taken over the leading position among the world's shipbuilding nations: sustained technological progress enables them to bypass some of the former leaders in the field. Another example is Sweden: its export industries thrive on technological lead in the making of certain quality products such as ballbearings, but in most kinds of Swedish industry the lead over the competitors in other countries is now no more than ten years' technological development.

The most fascinating part of this new competitive story is the increasing competition between firms which produce entirely different things. Aluminum companies compete with steel companies but also with forests and sawmills in the making of window frames and house siding. Factories making plastics compete with brass tube manufacturers, and indirectly with copper and zinc mines, but at the same time they also compete with farms and forests. The list could go on at any length.

Nor is there any escape from this situation without stifling progress. The new form of competition between alternative materials increases all the time and would only be accelerated by any attempts to stop it. For instance, if the tropical countries which produce natural rubber were to try to stop the downward drift of the prices of rubber by some kind of international price fixing, this would backfire on two counts. First, the synthetic-rubber factories would immediately be able to undersell the natural-rubber producers and capture a larger share of the market. Applying all their unused production capacity, these factories could already in the short run produce a larger quantity of rubber and at lower average cost. Some of the costs of production are fixed and are the same whether the factory works at or below full capacity, so the additional output at full-capacity production is cheaper and lowers average cost. Second, the synthetic-rubber industries would use some of the profits from expanded production as investment. They would invest in new plant and equipment and accelerate the expansion of their production. They would also use some of these profits for investing in more research and development to speed up the invention of even better and cheaper ways of substituting for natural rubber. To remain in production yet for some time, the tropical rubber farms have only one course of action left that is really viable: to meet the competition by keeping their prices on a level with those of the synthetics industries and to look for means of increasing their own productivity.

The same, of course, goes for all the various industries which produce materials which can substitute for each other. Synthetic rubber, by the way, is not one commodity but many, as is natural rubber. Fibers are even more diverse and specialized, and so on. All the many modern "synthetics" are really "processed materials," old stuff transformed by new and more ingenious technology. All this intensified processing of materials gives rise to or encourages competition on several levels. First there are many more basic raw material sources which compete for the same market. Second, factories and industrial firms are competing over a wider range. And then finally there is competition between the laboratories and the technico-scientific crews who discover the new formulas and work out the manufacturing procedures by which the new technology can be translated into industrial products.

Gadgets

The rising wave of substitution for raw materials is but one facet of the intensifying competition let loose by modern science-based technology. Another one is in alternative gadgets or processes that may supply the public's demands along essentially different technical routes. A big, trite case is in transportation: fly, drive, or ride a train – and, in the extreme case, go by ship? The railroads' competition with the airlines for medium-distance transportation is explicit – more so in Europe and Japan than in the United States. Their competition with truck transportation is partial but for that sake no less fierce, as one can see from the maneuverings of the "highway lobby" and despite combined solutions such as piggyback. Indirectly, then, factories making railroad equipment share the result of that competition. Competition between railroads and canals for freight hauling is an old story which exemplifies the same thing; but old as it is, it is still with us, on quite similar terms as before.

In daily traffic there is the competition between mass transit and the overflowing mass of individual cars. Neither has any absolute advantage over the other. The option to drive means freedom of route and timetable, but servitude under the wheel and the motor. The option to ride a mass transit means servitude under route and timetable but freedom from worry under way – the trip can be more leisure. Needless to say, the positive gains from individual driving are often frustrated by the very mass of people trying the same option. This competition is also two-faced: the car is needed to compete with the mass transit, but if it succeeds too well, this becomes its greatest failure.

We could go on mentioning any number of analogies, and there will be even more of them in the future. Houses can be built of almost anything, including steel and glass, or compressed garbage; and there are futurists anticipating buildings with walls made of forced warm air. The choice between alternative means for the heating of buildings becomes further complicated when insulation materials provide partial substitution between building materials and heating. In a similar way, there is partial substitution between heating and clothing. The do-it-yourself-er finds a choice between aluminum siding and periodic re-painting. Then there is eating out – in restaurants or picknick places – or we may choose to eat at home and still have the convenience of ready-cooked food in cans and packages. When we write, we can use typewriter instead of longhand, and then we are back again to longhand for memos to be reproduced by xerox in the desired number of copies, not to mention automatic print-outs from words spoken into a dictation machine. There is any number of methods for reproducing documents to replace conventional printing. The mail and the telegraph have been partial substitutes for each other for some time, and then came the telephone, the teleprinter, and the closed-circuit television to form a complex display of alternative possibilities for long-distance messages. In a similar way, there is competition and partial substitution between mass media: between moviehouse and television, between radio and grammophone, and so on. The new possibilities of storing radio and television programs on tape merely underscore this competition. Meanwhile, traditional live performance of theatre and concerts continue within limits, the mass media have not substituted for them entirely. The recent mass rallies at music festivals promise that live performance will not disappear either.

It is characteristic that new gadgets tend to substitute in part only for the old ones. Many alternatives retain a safe minimum field of application while large border areas are up for grabs for the producers who are the most vigorous and creative. Such alternatives have their advantages and disadvantages which are not all measured in money; the choice among them is often a combination of cost and comfort.

One of today's risks is that some competitors may give up too early. We see an example in the death of mass transit systems where the public finds itself stranded with fewer options. If the public lets it happen, a gap of information is usually to blame.

Purposes

All of this technological substitution should keep competition alive for a long time. Overshadowing it is however another set of factors: people are getting more of a chance to choose between entirely different purposes when they spend their money. As people's consumption moves from penury to affluence, it becomes less and less predictable what different goods they will buy.

On a low level of per-capita income, people's spending is fairly predictable. Within limits, it is also predictable how people's spending will change when their incomes change moderately. When it comes to food consumption, such a pattern of spending was discovered more than a hundred years ago by a German statistician named Ernst Engel; after him it is called Engel's law. What the law says is quite simple: as incomes rise, a smaller and smaller percentage is spent on food. Evidently, if one is very poor, a large part of his income must be used to buy the minimum amount of food without which he cannot survive. As he gets higher income, he will eat more and better, but his spending on food will increase slower than the total of his outlay for other things. After a point, he can hardly eat more, only better. When all physiological needs for calories, proteins and vitamins are met, he can still keep increasing the aesthetic quality (as he sees it) of his food. This may mean more luxury foods, and people indulging in fancy delicacies can go quite some way spending money in this manner. Experience shows, however, that most people become more interested in other things, and even the richest gourmet usually spends only a small fraction of what he has on food, drink, and excitants.

The same principle as for food can be traced also for other necessities of life. At low income levels the necessities take up most of people's budget in certain proportions which seem to be characteristic of the time and place. After a somewhat decent level of living has been reached, the individual becomes more and more free in his choice to spend his money without having to follow any set pattern. He gets the option to choose certain luxuries to the complete neglect of some other luxuries.

Sheer necessity is less than most people think. Instructive here is the famous anecdote about the Greek philosopher Diogenes who asked King Alexander to step out of the sun for him – no greater favor was needed by a thinker who lived in a barrel. We must remember that when people spend and consume above the level of sheer physical necessity, they are inspired by other motives. These motives may be aesthetic, moral, or religious, or a combination of all of them. All three categories must be taken in a wide sense. The "moral" includes the immoral as well as the programmatically anti-moral. The religious covers the quasi-religious and also the believingly anti-religious. The "moral" also includes the feeling for power and other morale building elements of a culture. The "aesthetic" means not only what ordinary people find beautiful or ugly. There is also the intellectual or professional specialist appeal. The mathematical minded may find beauty in an abstract thought, and a surgeon may find it in a typical tumor. Then there are also all sorts of outrights perversions which attract certain minds whether the rest of us like it or not.

The new and unprecedented fact about the affluent society is now this, that luxuries – the things people can live without – are taking up a major part, and a steadily growing part, of all the production and consumption. And this can only make competition more and more intense. Bread and bricks and shoesoles used to have a guaranteed market. But the goods that have guaranteed markets are not only less secure, because of substitution; they are also a dwindling fraction of the total economy. The luxuries are not merely a large component of today's economic life in the rich countries, they also make up a growing share of an expanding economy. The competitive thrust from the luxuries is therefore accelerating, at the same time as this too is compounded by the possibilities of substitution. In old-fashioned competition, bad bakeries and brickmakers could lose out to better bakeries and brickmakers. But in modern competition, bad movies and tedious concerts and indifferent religious preachers and nondescript wines risk to lose out, not merely to better variants of their own kind but to entirely different kinds of luxuries. "I am just giving up on television" is the type of reaction which really may hurt an industry and not just shift the competitive advantage among the firms of that industry.

The intensified competition makes for a more volatile economy and society. We can see this clearly in the growing field of recreation – growing because people have more time on their hands and more money to spend. Recreation is not only another name for leisure. In fact it is a collective label for a major part of all modern luxuries. And here the competition is growing at an accelerating pace as people are given many options of different kinds of recreation. There are the indoors and the outdoors types of recreation, the active and the contemplative, the sensual and the spiritual, in any number of variants. This is how it happens that our car manufacturer competes with the stereo plant, and the church, and the spiritist salon, and the "encounter groups" (with more or less competent psychiatric guidance), and all of them compete with sporting goods' stores (and their manufacturers, and their raw-material suppliers) and football stadiums and professional boxing rings and numbers games. Literally thousands of possible forms of recreation are calling for our money in a crescendo of competition which is limited but not mitigated by the amount of time a person has – not to mention his physical and mental capacity to engage in any or all of these many competing activities.

In practice competition is limited also by social inertia and people's tendency to imitate each other. Some industries also use political lobbying to give themselves a larger share of the market than they deserve. In such ways, some of our options may be foreclosed for us. And foreclosing one option may force the foreclosing of others, as we shall see in more detail later.

News and entertainment

When we are getting so much more free time and options for recreation, a large part of the gains is captured by the mass media. The modern media represent of course an enormously enlarged capacity to transmit, but at the same time they are able to draw on a continuously expanding multitude of sources for news and entertainment.

The only reason to mention the ease and rapidity of diffusion by radio and television is because most people get so accustomed to them that they may cease reflecting on it. And the economic difficulties of newspapers tend to obscure the fact that to consumers they are much cheaper than ever before. And for those who are fed up with the troika of national television networks, the promise of more cable television (CATV) and "bandwidth compression" means a future smorgasbord of unlimited variations.

And they have every chance of becoming unlimited. Other technologi-

cal progress, in transportation and in storage of data, gives the program-
mers the challenge of intensifying world wide competition between news,
ideas, art and whatever.

High productivity in data storage began in the fifteenth century with
the printing press. It expanded with the coming of photography: micro-
film, microfiche and microdots. Then there are grammophone records,
tape recordings of all descriptions and, among the latest, the computer
memories. The cost per unit of data is now almost incredibly small.

Transportation we need hardly elaborate upon. Within the "global
village," geographical distances have shrunk so much that if the rock
festival is in a hurry, it can be in Tokyo tomorrow. Unless you ask for
cultural understanding; for in that dimension, the world is still much
larger than you think. The celebrated American folk singer who came
to Japan with her message of peace and international understanding was
quickly cooled off by Japanese etiquette. So, the whole world's news
sources, culture and politics are at our fingertips. But not necessarily within our mental grasp. The whole world may be watching, but do they see
what we see?

Oldfashioned newscasters still insist that they convey facts and nothing
but facts. They still rest in the comfortable bygone days when the West
and its ideology was all that counted, and the bias of one's own tacit assumptions was overlooked. With the increasing world-wide variety of
news sources, a younger generation of reporters and broadcasters has been
overwhelmed by the experience that objectivity in news release is not possible. The way out, they feel, is that the reporter should voice his own
opinion and in the free market place of ideas truth should eventually
emerge from the chorus of voices. They also say that the broadcaster can
not be a mere tape recorder of his time and its happenings. But how does
he arrive at his own opinion? If he does not know that, he risks to be an
unknown master's voice. To be able to analyze the sources of his own
opinions and attitudes, he must first be aware of the problems. This free
market place of ideas is by no means a parochial place. The global village
harbors a game of national and international ideas, purposes, opinions,
and cultures. News is released within this continuously shifting cultural
framework. And the different audiences will understand the meaning of
the news in the degree as the news appeals to the "right" or "wrong" in
their own civilization's values. The more creative this game with cultural
values – the more successful and well-paid the news announcer and the
more entertaining the news. Let us take as an example the death of President John Kennedy. To Americans, it was the doing of a single deranged

mind. Sophisticated European public opinion assumed a conspiracy. The Byzantine tradition of conspiracy and political manipulation loomed in newspaper headlines with Archbishop Makarios, the Cypriot statesman, volunteering the opinion that the Kennedy murder was engineered by his successor.

When a newscaster insists that his news is just "a guide to our world that day" and that he is not taking sides or is responsible for the news' effect on the public he is innocent about the creative function of his own job. No factual news can be broadcast without involving appeals to public attitudes at the same time. And this may have nothing to do with the individual newscaster's direct intentions. For one thing, the very limitation of time in broadcasting and space in printing implies a selection which inevitably becomes a bias, as every reporter knows. Then a fact gets meaning in communication only when it is combined with our community values and their positive or negative character. This combination makes not only a news item entertaining but is also a key to the kind of public response a piece of news gets. This can happen in two ways. Either the facts can be reported together with conspicuous, positive or negative references well known to the community. And these references clearly tell at once whether the news should be good or bad for the society. This explicit case is rare in a democracy of western type. The obvious value references are more common as indoctrination in dictatorships. For instance, an astronout may step out from his space ship and announce after an orbital trip: This has been achieved thanks to Comrade X and his successful administration united in collaboration with the victorious glorious peace loving Y people.

The more usual way to release news in a democracy is represented by his colleague in a different country after his orbital journey. Well knowing that his audience puts a tremendous value on speed and excitement wherever they go, he could cut down his communication to a laconic explanation: Man what a ride!

In such a case the news itself is such an established positive or negative social value in the community that a mere reference to it elicits the corresponding reaction from the public. Or to take a homespun example: When the Illini baseball players lose their game no colorful value references are needed to make this bad news in Illinois and good news wherever the other team is at home. On another level: in peacetime the mere fact of any airplane or naval disaster is bad news anywhere, but during World War II, the mere fact of the sinking of the German battle ship "Bismarck" was good news in England.

These principles of communication are primitive, and old as the pyramids. No one has even proved as yet any difference between the principles of mass communication and of individual dialog. Madison Avenue often feels that they have invented the principles they use, whether they try to sell a soap or a President. The difference in communication between our age and that of Benjamin Franklin or Louis XI or the Tower of Babel is not in the principles of communication but in the larger multitude of news sources and competing ideologies. This modern multitude cannot be wished away by the saying that people are the same everywhere.

The intensifying competition in the free market of news and ideas is made still more intensive by the expanding access to the culture of all peoples on earth. Japanese theater and Uzbek ballet and genuine Watusi and pre-paleolithic ceremonies from the jungles of Brazil all get stored on magnetic tape or programmed through satellites and broadcast into our living rooms in a matter of minutes. The onrush of the whole wide world brings along more than the trimmings and spectacles of the culture we can see and hear. The religions, the ideologies, the styles of life of India, the Philippines, Madagascar and the Micronesian islands are all beginning to be taken serious as alternatives to Judaeo-Christian tradition. Today, Elmer Gantry competes not only with Baptists and Episcopalians but also with the guru's and the Maoists and the Soka Gakkai and a host of other live spirits. In past ages the Occident could play with exotic things; in the eighteenth century, the East India Companies in Europe inspired a long-lived fashion trend in imitating Chinese art in architecture, furniture and paintings and, most durably of all, in "China ware." But these were cultural loans into a solidly integrated Christian civilization. Only in our time are the different cultures around the globe in competition for real to replace each other.

The *embarras de richesse* of all these global options is made even more bewildering because rising affluence the world over permits more individuals in each country to become creative in their culture. In ages of penury, most of the potential geniuses died from malnutrition in childhood or were muffled by social prejudice. For instance, the rich Brazilian literature begins now to be of concern to others outside the country than just the high-brow Nobel Prize Committee. But this expanding wealth of options in a single field may tend to capture the individual's interest and limit his involvement with other options of the world.

In contrast to commodity production, the productivity of culture as such has not increased at all. With all the technical gadgets, it does not take less time today to create a novel than it did in the age of the goose feather. But of course there are so many more producers at work. In fact, they are so numerous that they may even reduce each other's productivity – considering the amount of staff and time that goes into a single movie or television show.

There is a real risk that our complete access to all kinds of options, as seems to become possible in cable television, will be used for choice of too many variations or repetitions of old interests and familiar features. It already happens in many smalltown newspapers. How many options people have is one thing and how many they really want is something else again. One can only lead a horse to the water, one can not force him to drink. Then, does our education prepare us for all these new options? Or will we in our choice be like children in school who choose the subjects that seem to require the least effort? If this is what we do, we are soon back to the parochial closed community and the global village becomes a ghost town.

Competition within firms and bureaucracies

It is hardly news any more to say that a modern corporation is far from "monolithic" when it comes to making economic decisions. Already the competition for rapid promotion between vice presidents, junior executives, and engineers lends a competitive aspect to the American corporation. This aspect is perhaps as yet less striking in Europe. The feature is reported to be absent in Japan, at least on the surface – there may be other rewards specific to Japanese culture which escape a Westerner. In the USSR, the bureaucracies – both technological and political – are in themselves extremely competitive in the race for promotion. It is another matter that much of their competition takes the form of avoiding mistakes by getting ensconced in routine.

The internal competition within the American corporation is intensified because the firm cannot escape the competition between substitute products. The attempted escape from the squeeze of product competition is in "product diversification." This can be done in two different ways. One is if a firm begins to produce its own substitutes, as for instance if a steel firm were to buy up an aluminum company. Another is to acquire interests in entirely different activities, as a means of securing income from a diversity of sources. A television network may buy a professional football league, and an already bankrupt railroad tries to invest in various things among them television stations. This explains the recent snowballing of "conglomerates": huge corporations integrating numerous firms which make several different kinds of products. The public and the politicians seem to believe that the formation of conglomerates leads to less competition, and maybe that is the intention of those who build the conglomerates. More to the point, the conglomerates are a symptom of how fierce the competition already is. What the conglomerates try to do is to mitigate the competition. To the extent they succeed in this, they do so by internalizing the competition – making it an affair within the same firm. Such internalized competition still has to fight over alternative new products, or what emphasis to place on various lines of production. The substitutions of materials and gadgets that we have talked about, and the wider choice of luxuries we have as consumers, are more powerful forces than any corporate organizations in a free country which may try to limit competition.

Options for jobs and careers
Even long after leaving high school or college, more people have more career options today than ever before. Many may have the feeling that I have had it and there are no other options. Many of them have a case because of discrimination or sometimes bad luck. But there are many who have not sat down and taken a hard look at their options, or maybe they have themselves decided to foreclose further options for one reason or another.

The expansion of options is not as simple as it sounds, either. Those who get trained in the first place for doing one thing and then wind up doing something more or less different, are more numerous than ever. Not just because the population of the world and of nearly every country is larger than ever; but they are more numerous also in relation to the rest of the population. This has to do with the fact that more people than ever before hold qualified jobs, positions requiring advanced training and more than manual routine skills. In itself this would open up more options, for the skilled have always had more to choose from than traditional peasants or routine drudgery workers. Under modern conditions there are also more and more occupations where some basic competence in science and technology will qualify an individual to handle several different types of work, possibly with some modicum of on-the-job training. It is not only middle-aged housewives who nowadays begin to question sincerely their line of work. Surprisingly high up in mature middle age, more people than ever leave their initial choice of livelihood and opt for something else which is not too remote from their professional and everyday skills. More people are moving between universities, politics, government bureaucracy, business, and the free professions, than would have been thought of a generation ago. More engineers become businessmen, more lawyers go into one business or another, economic statisticians become industry analysts of technical coefficients; foremen in one line of factory industry go into another one; individuals with profitable skills take up another trade, maybe because they want to move to another part of the country; and so on.

All right, say the many who discover no options for themselves, so what is that to me? In some direct or indirect way, it has consequences for most people. It means, for instance, that employers are more than ever on their toes for not losing qualified staff. They do not have to risk losing all their attractive employees to become wary; if a firm is deserted by ten per cent of its qualified staff, that might spell disaster. The mobile ones, those who are capable and strong enough to pull up their roots and go elsewhere, need not be overwhelmingly numerous to bring in the fresh air of competition. Such episodes are a warning to the leadership of bureaucracies and universities as well as industry and trade that employees can not be taken for granted. To fight against shortsighted employers, labor mobility could be a more efficient weapon than strikes. Even those who stay put will benefit, unless they show their hand.

Those are the possibilities in the optional society. They may not be obvious in a year of recession, but then recessions are not what progress is made of. More serious threats to the free options are discrimination because of "race," sex and other similar reasons, and the quasi bondage of modern pension funds.

A great deal has been written about discrimination, but mainly to defend the victims of prejudice. Much less has been said about the great losses to society as a whole which because of prejudices loses the options to recruit the best talent for each job. Those favored by discrimination are almost by definition the second best. A prejudiced society will at length hurt itself so much that it loses out in competition with the rest of the world.

The pension funds are a more puzzling problem. On the face of it, they may appear as a great step of social progress. They have created large accumulations of wealth which no one can touch, except as beneficiaries who draw pensions from the annual income of this wealth. This "para-proprietal" arrangement has been likened to the "grand domain" of the Middle Ages (Father Harbrecht). The comparison is to the point: the Mediaeval "grand domain" was a large estate offering a livelihood to all who had a right to live there – but that was the only place in the world where those people could live in security. In a similar way, the beneficiaries of the large industrial pension fund are tied to their corporation in a kind of modern bondage. Their options are foreclosed, the competition for them on the labor market has been eliminated.

CHAPTER IV

ODDS AGAINST EQUALITY: THE COMPETITION FOR MONEY, FREEDOM AND POWER

When nobody is perfect, at least competition is less imperfect than at any time in the past. And of course it can be further improved. The optional society makes people compete for the distribution of income. First, the distribution within a society – between its rich, its middle classes and its poor. Second, the distribution between countries, between the rich, the middle-income, and the poor countries.

Before discussing the distribution of conventional income, let us say at once that income is much more than money. Money is not an end in itself; it is a means to getting whatever we want out of life. And that covers a good deal more than bread and shelter. The luxuries of all time have included many forms of "psychic income." Among these are freedom, prestige, power, and the access to news and entertainment. That these are "economic goods" is clear because people are willing to pay money for them. How these psychic incomes are distributed in society gives a large part of the meaning of the distribution of money incomes.

Let us first take a look at the *distribution of money income* within a country. At any given time, and in the very short run, total income in a country is a comparatively fixed sum. How total money income is distributed between people in a country may sometimes influence the growth of the size of total income in the country, but this may happen mainly in the longer run. It is a different matter that people who use their money carefully will get more out of it than will the careless. In the short run, from one year to the next, the distribution of income can only slightly affect the total there is to distribute.

There are some basic facts to nail down. One of them is that incomes are always unequally distributed, at least in societies with any degree of specialization and division of labor. That has always been so, still is, and the prospect is for the same to go on to some extent. Even Swedish Socialists are modest enough to strive merely for "more equality" in their income distribution. There are good reasons why some degree of inequality is desirable as an element of competition between individuals – desirable, that is, to secure the best use of talent in society.

The degree of inequality is usually less extreme in the affluent nations of North America and western Europe than in the low-income underdeveloped countries. However, Europe in its past days of mass poverty had more inequality than at present. The Communist parts of the world come in a separate category. Their programmatic equality is not put in practice partly because of "stakhanovism" and other features of a favoritist system. More important, some of the psychic income is there severely rationed in the interest of political discipline. One of the most limited economic goods – power – is almost entirely in the hands of a small class in society, the monopoly Party.

The prevalence of economic inequality in advanced societies requires some explanation. Traditional tribal society in Black Africa displays essential equality between people, and so do some other even more archaic societies here and there in the world such as the natives of New Guinea. This archaic equality belongs to an old phase in economic history, a phase which was before the coming of economies with specialization and division of labor. It is typical also that even in Black Africa, this primitive equality appears to be breaking up under the pressure of modern economic development. Archaic equality existed at a terrible price. Such a community was at the mercy both of nature and of hostile tribes. Primitive equality has nothing in common with modern tendencies in the affluent societies. People who do not understand primitive mankind sometimes believe it a model to follow in modern time.

Progress from tribal to somewhat more advanced economic organization gave rise to sharp class divisions within society. The early great civilizations, as in Egypt, Babylonia, China and Peru, relied on large irrigation works. That required an elaborate organization of society, with privileged classes in its command positions. The coming of mining enterprises, since the Bronze Age, added more reasons for complex administration and brought on classical slavery. Since those days, the distribution of incomes in most societies has been highly unequal. Any large organized country living on low-productive means still needed a central authority. The elites in power would regularly ask for economic as well as other privileges. From the priests of Egypt and Peru to the mandarins of imperial China, all large organized societies had their rich, often superrich, classes. Such a distribution of income in societies of penury may to some extent have been necessary to create and maintain a leisured class.

In such societies only a class of leisure could devote their minds and their time to inventions and other advanced cultural pursuits – all of which, in the long run, was supposed to benefit also the toiling masses. Just as often, of course, the leisured classes would take the cake and eat it and walk away without producing anything worth-while. Intermittent revolts, in Europe and China and elsewhere, would at times give voice to the exasperated poor. Such a *révolte de la misère* could for a while throw a fragile society to pieces. Usually it provoked a reconstruction of the old system leaving it more powerful than ever. The Communist revolution in Russia is a typical case where the masses rose against authorities who were more ineffectual than they were oppressive. The state that Lenin built learnt the lesson.

Marxian theory insists that inequality of income increases as capitalistic economic development runs its course. The catastrophy which was predicted on such grounds has not come, however, which is the main case where Marxian theory has failed in real life. It is likely that inequality of income increased in late phases of pre-capitalistic development, as in imperial China. Maybe it did so too in some very early phases of capitalism in Europe. But the trend turned, in part because of influence from America where common people got higher incomes than in the Old world in the early period of industrialism. Already nineteenth century England – a class society if there ever was one – saw rising levels of living among common workers.

In detail, the process is by no means clear. The fact remains that the capitalistic, later the mixed or semi-socialistic development in Europe led to a gradual reduction of the inequality in incomes.

In the United States, these inequalities are less striking than in most other countries. The United States of today is essentially a middle-class country. The vast majority of all families have incomes relatively close to the average. Only small fractions of the population live very far below or very far above this average. In affluent America, genuine poverty still exists, but the poor are definitely a minority. A major part of the population enjoys something rather close to equality of income and opportunity. This relative equality is the most pronounced in the cities of the East, the Midwest and the West. In the South, there is more inequality, even when white and black people are counted separately. The reasons are not only in discrimination and its indirect impact upon the whole fabric of society. There is also unequal property distribution, especially in the cotton plantation areas. The aristocratic heritage in the Deep South made it a more unequal society, and also caused it to lag behind the rest of the country in economic development.

The distribution of landed wealth has a tendency to remain unchanged over long periods which prolongs the effect of past inequalities. A radical land reform – which re-distributes land ownership to make it more equitable between the many who work the land – should have been done in the Deep South around 1870 or 1880. This could have laid the foundations of a sounder society. The Hayes Compromise gave the upper hand to the shortsighted class egoism of the large landowners. Latin America abounds with similar examples, only more extreme. In those countries the precious option to move toward a modern society is time and again blocked by resistance against land reform which still reflects class egoism at its most destructive – no matter how many economic fallacies are mustered to defend the interests of the idle rich.

But the affluent society becomes highly optional when it favors social mobility by its wider diffusion of income. It still may be more an advantage than a handicap to come from a rich family. It follows however, when decent incomes are within the reach of most people that a large part of all economic and social advancement must go to middle-income groups, that is to the majority. Therefore the recruitment for qualified jobs and above-average incomes has less tendency to be limited to certain groups than in societies of penury where the differences between the social classes are much sharper.

Reasons for the degree of equality

How can we explain that there is more equality of incomes in an advanced industrial state? Essentially, it is because both the ways of production and the conditions of supply and demand require relative equality in incomes.

First there are the ways of production. It was possible to pay factory workers very low wages when their jobs were simple and they were easy to replace. "Machine work is easy," said one of the early economists of capitalist persuasion quoted by Marx. That was true once upon a time, but not today. Modern machines are complicated and demand a good deal of competence from the operators. The "proletarians" of early capitalist days could not have been trusted to handle the highly sophisticated factories and offices of modern America, Europe, Japan, and the USSR. Such people would be physically unfit as well as culturally and mentally unprepared. They would also lack motivation to be accurate in operation and maintenance of the complicated machines. Without enough skill and accuracy, the complicated machinery would not make sense and would break down prematurely. A worker's pay scale stands in some relation to the economic risk of the firm. Without the incentive of substantial wages, the firm could not attract and hold the right caliber of workers. Substandard workers would jeopardize the security of high-priced equipment and risk turning out shoddy goods.

Supply and demand in mass consumption also call for a degree of equality in incomes. Modern industry is at its most productive when it turns out goods in large quantities. The merchandise does not have to be as standardized as was once the case. Automated factories can give a surprising degree of variation even to cars and household appliances produced in huge series. Mass production makes sense only if there is mass consumption. Even so, this does not prevent the width of options in modern society. The articles that can be and are mass produced are so numerous that no standardized pattern of consumption is called for, as it was in the days of H. G. Wells. The role of mass consumption is still essential. Total demand for all kinds of goods will be the largest when many individuals have substantial means. The point was once one of the highlights of socialist theory when the crises of a capitalist economy were explained as "over production." However, already in the early nineteenth century, the French economist Say insisted that there is no such thing as over-production, only under-consumption ("Say's law.") We may add, by way of explanation, that there might also be lopsided production causing consumer demand for some goods to be over-supplied while others remain unsatisfied. This happens in fact more often under socialism than in countries where industrialists are profit conscious and profit trained.

The central fact remains that mass production will make sense on condition that there is also mass consumption. This happens in the degree that incomes are widely distributed. A society with sharp class divisions would demand less mass goods. A class society would demand more of the luxuries which cater to individual taste of the rich and require more hand labor and less machine work. An aristocratic society therefore would make less use of the specific advantages of modern industrial mass production. At length, therefore, it would produce less profits too. Union wage demands and the threat of strikes do their part to accelerate the redistribution of incomes. But basically modern industry leaders have learnt the lesson first taught by Henry Ford: pay the workers well enough and they become customers for the goods they help to produce.

The degree of equality in modern America has also been helped by the background of relative equality in the farmer communities. In most of the country, the Federal domain was once converted into private property in ways which favored the creation of even-sized farms.

This society of qualified workers with high mass consumption presents two sets of problems both related to each other. One is: how much equality should we want to have – either because we already have it or because we want to move toward it? So far, the relative equality we have has been for the good. A modern economy can not live with a high degree of inequality, as found in penury societies. Then, should equality be pushed farther than it has in a country such as the United States, and if that is what we want, where should we stop? At some point, extreme equality might have adverse effects. It might blunt incentives and fail to allocate talent to the jobs where it does the most good. Can superior talent be persuaded to produce its best merely by recognition for superior performance? Maybe it happens in school but in real life we have not sufficient reason to take it for granted. Money seems necessary at least as a partial inducement if society is to get the best out of its talent. Placing talented people where they belong also means keeping the less talented away from positions where they might do harm by their incompetence. But just what degree of equality of income that would maximize social productivity, that seems to be something we have not yet explored.

The other question is about the extremes of the income distribution – the very rich and the very poor. Despite its relative equality, income distribution in modern America still leaves many people abjectly poor and allows quite a few to become super-rich. It is doubtful that any society needs to have either, and the affluent society certainly has the options to upgrade its poor and to curtail its super-rich.

Let us first explain why we are saying that both the very poor and the very rich, in the United States, are more numerous than they would be as a consequence of the general economic system. The distribution of income and wealth among people usually follows certain patterns. The number of people who have an income, say, from $ 6000 to $ 8000 is a number which stands in a certain proportion to the number of those who have, for instance, between $ 8000 and $ 10 000. Looking at this proportion, one can roughly foresee how many people have between $ 10 000 and $ 12 000, between $ 12 000 and $ 14 000, and so on. The proportions between numbers of people who have certain income levels form a consistent system. This is called a *distributive function* and in some way it reflects the chances people have to advance within their society. Especially in small-town states such as Maine and Montana with no large metropolitan centers the actual distribution often closely reflects such a precise pattern. How equal or unequal the distribution is, that again varies between parts of the country as it does between parts of the world. In general the South has less equality in the income distribution than other parts of the United States. But in the country as a whole, and especially in the large-city areas, there are two deviations from a distributive function. There are two sets of figures which can not be foreseen from the rest of the distribution. These are the numbers of the very poor and the very rich: The slums and the stars.

The very rich

The very rich appear nearly always to be somewhat more numerous than we should expect from the proportions between the other income groups. There is more income going to people in very high income brackets than would be reasonable to expect from free competition in an affluent society. This deviation from the distributive function we call the "star effect."

Look for instance at the star performers of the movies and of television. Their individual incomes appear out of line with the kind of work they do. Many movie stars are far from remarkable, even in the art they perform. Out there, among the general public, there are literally thousands upon thousands of men and women who are at least as talented as the stars on the screen. But those people were never recruited for a movie career. Why, then, has the movie industry so long continued to pay star salaries when just as good pictures could be produced with far lower wages? The potential supply of human talent in the performing arts is actually larger than the demand at its present price; why, then, does the price climb so high?

The answer to this puzzle is in a peculiar type of restriction on competition: because of shortage of room on the stage. The public's attention span is limited, especially when the public is still immature enough to worship idols among the actors and actresses to whom it pays attention. You can not have too many gods in one Pantheon or too many saints in one cathedral. This makes it essential for the movie companies to build up attention to star performers rather than to the drama they are supposed to communicate. The supply cost of stars becomes inflated by the very mechanism of stardom: a star, to have the box-office effect of an idol, needs the build-up of publicity, and that costs money. Once the industry has invested in a star, the risk is great that such a highly appreciated asset will go to another company. So the market value of a star becomes inflated to a level far above the original supply cost of equivalent or even superior talent. A shortage has been created artificially; a shortage of commercially available talent.

The individual who gets to stardom has of course been lucky. In most cases he has been elevated far beyond the normal market value of his talent, training, and hard work.

And so it goes, with variations, in most of the occupations with very high incomes. The entertainment world is only the most conspicuous arena. Business leadership is a similar case. There is an artificial shortage, created by the power of vested interest, including the interest of sons and in-laws. President Kennedy was so right; life is unfair. Inherited wealth is of course a good start in business. With or without it, those who once were admitted to a career in business leadership with some measure of success are more likely to advance than are the numerous potential executives who were never recruited for such positions. Another case in point are the high-fee law firms, as on New York's Wall Street, which can almost guarantee that their attorneys will get rich. They are a more or less closed shop resembling the crafts' guilds of the Middle Ages. Out in the small towns, numerous lawyers are just as bright, but most of them never happened to place their feet inside a Wall Street office.

An interesting theme in American film drama which pops up quite frequently is the "discovery" of *the* talent. Here the film makers love to glorify the stars of the entertainment world more often than the top successes in other professions. But that is due to a mixture of ignorance and inflated ego. The question is if drama about life is not more arresting than drama about drama. The typical plot shows the budding star when she is manipulated forward to the accidental attention of some high brass who "just happens to drop in there." The implicit admission is too obvious: stardom depends on luck.

It is perhaps in politics that the star system reveals its hollowness altogether. Leading politicians have to be built up as much as any movie star. But so many nobodies have come from obscurity to high office over night, usually by default. After that they have done as well, or sometimes better than, the leading politicians built up by the publicity that only money and vested interests can buy. How much excellent leadership is in fact latent among the rank and file? Harry Truman and Margaret Chase Smith emerged from the rank and files and became among those most highly regarded, but American politics is replete with analogies at all levels. Yet the game of politics still requires the build-up of publicity. Just as in business and the entertainment world, high talent is not scarce, but the options to use it are restricted.

The star system's hold on the public is of course related to common people's idol worship and attention span. With increasing education and more maturity of taste and judgment among the public the options are expanding. It is a healthy sign that the star systems are weakening. The stars of movie and television screens tend to become more and more short-lived, and the political machines are beginning to break up. More discrimination – more sense for options – will eventually bring down even more of the star system. This is healthy, for with more options we can expect more excellence in performance when we do not have to put up with the inflated egos of those who take their stardom for granted.

Middle-income people have to earn their way by talent, training, and hard work. When the "stars" owe much of their high incomes to a fourth dimension – namely, luck – then there are good reasons to correct their exceptional incomes. The graduated income tax, which has been decried in many quarters for some presumed unfairness, can very well be justified as a tax on luck. To use it for curbing the accumulation of extreme riches has nothing unfair about it. Up to some point, decided by economic analysis and common sense, the tax on luck is altogether reasonable. It may not be necessary to abolish all high incomes. The tax might be graduated in such a way that the number of rich people, and the amount of their riches, are brought down to what would follow from the general competitive relations in society. This would merely eliminate the "star effect" from the distribution of income and wealth, it would not take away all strong economic incentives in a free society.

The poor in America

The poor in America are an even deeper problem. They, too, are more numerous in the United States than we would expect from the general competitive relations in this country. Of course there are some never-do-well individuals in any society; even such a welfare state as Sweden has some very poor people – at least some of them by voluntary choice. The hippies can not blame their poverty on society either. But the very poor in America are much too numerous, and this has been said many times. They represent an unbalance in society. If this is corrected, there will be more freedom in all parts of society. Not only for those who are poor now who will be able to join the optional society. But also for the rest of us. Society as a whole will become more optional too when there will be no large blocks of inert, undeveloped people getting in the way of free human choices. For instance, there will be less need to fear the slums or the streets after dark. When the poor get more options, so do the rest of us.

There are specific reasons why the very poor in America are more numerous than we expect from the general picture. Why just those individuals are in that class of people often depends on a characteristic "slum effect." Their bad luck is not always individual, as the good luck of the stars. The misery is perhaps even more often acquired through birth and growing up in slums – urban slums or rural slums. The "culture of poverty" (Oscar Lewis) foredooms many of the slum's offspring to remain in the vicious circle of their native environment. The problem is made worse in America because of the parochial neighborhood mentality in much of American social life, and also because of the naiveté of our laws against "sin." Gambling and dope are moral evils, but they only thrive on the attempts at fighting mere symptoms. Just as under Prohibition, the laws against gambling and narcotics get big money to the captains of organized crime, recruit their agents and henchmen, increase the number of addicts by organized pushing, and turn harmless addicts into robbers. The slum areas are the most helpless in the grip of this organized evil which misguided idealism has given a chance to thrive.

The ideology of the neighborhood school may wave the flag of free choice but in fact it is the opposite – a foreclosing of options – for all parties concerned. Those who oppose school integration and busing of students deny the slum children the right to try a fresh start and break away from the trap in which their elders got stuck.

Then the slum areas also tend to have higher birth rates than the country at large. Our kind of welfare system keeps all these people alive and encourages them to have large families. At the same time these people are not getting any chance ever to be anything else than they are. If this is to drag on, the slum centers will be a permanent, deprived segment of society, gradually growing, occupying more and more of its space, degrading ever larger numbers of its people and threatening the very life of a free society. There is no good reason why this should be so. Our society has its options. The means are there if they are only used.

When the level of income rises in a society, people's incomes tend in general to become more equal. Obviously it is easier to change the distribution when there is more income to go around.

Productivity and incomes

If incomes become more equal in a society, this does not always reflect changes in productivity. There is a widespread misconception – in America and elsewhere – that workers deserve higher wages to the extent their industry has become more productive. Union wage demands often take rising company profits as a reason for their workers to get higher pay. When productivity in a specific industry goes up, should not this be a good reason for wages to go up more or less in proportion to the productivity gain?

No, that reasoning is all wrong. If it did happen that way, the industries with rising productivity would attract more than their share of the labor force. They would then either be oversupplied with workers – which in the normal course of events would depress wages again – or else the unions in those industries would have to resort to closed-shop tactics. Such tactics would create new class barriers in a society and would make incomes more unequal.

On the other hand, in occupations and industries where there are no productivity gains, wages would not go up at all. These occupations would dwindle away for lack of recruitment, or they would be filled with extremely low-paid people who have no chance to enter the closed-shop unions in the industries with high and rising wages.

Some of this actually happens in America, but fortunately not all the time. But if it is a mistake for workers in industries with sharp rises in productivity to grab their apparent share of this growth – what should be done instead? A good example is set by agriculture production in America, one of the most competitive industries in the world. Agricultural production includes the work of the farmers and of the industries which supply them with production inputs such as machines and chemicals. Since thirty or forty years, American agricultural production has scored higher measurable productivity gains than most manufacturing industries in the country – in any event higher than the national economy as a whole. But despite price supports, farmers' incomes have not risen faster than incomes in general; instead they have increased at a similar pace as the general income level. The difference – agriculture's extraordinary gains in productivity – has been passed on to the consuming public. The raw materials for our food cost the consumers less in real terms – that is in terms of how many hours people have to work to pay for them. Many consumers will not readily believe this, but it is true. Of course long-term inflation creates some optical illusions about prices then and now. And the price of food depends on more than farmers. It seems for instance that the food processing industries, and food marketing, have not improved their productivity as much as farmers have.

The gain made by specific productivity growth in agricultural production are made to benefit society at large. These gains are of course created by many social forces in concert, not just by the farmers' increasing skill in management and dexterity at handling equipment. Eventually the farmers themselves also pay lower real prices for their food. They and others also share in the gains from rising productivity in other industries, to the extent these gains spill over to the public in general. Rising productivity in other industries is also stimulated by the lower real cost of food which their workers have to pay.

The lesson may be hard to get through to union men. But social justice and domestic tranquillity are not the only reasons why society needs a distribution of incomes which may be different from the result of a hard-bargaining contest between workers' wage demands and capitalists' profits. If productivity goes up more than average for the country in, say, the automobile industry, it does not follow that excess earnings have to be divided between workers and shareholders. Since the gains in productivity come from many parts of society, it is perfectly reasonable that the excess earnings should be passed on to the general public by lower prices of cars, for instance. This will to some extent benefit also the automobile workers – and the investors in the industry – most of them buy cars themselves. In a still more indirect way, these same workers and investors will also profit by the fact that lower prices of what they produce will contribute toward keeping down the price increases of still other classes of goods and services.

The really difficult problems of adjustment come from those industries and services in which productivity does not go up, or at least not as fast as in the country as a whole. They have to raise their prices or reduce their volume of activity, maybe disappear entirely. Without raising their prices, such industries cannot pay wages that will hold their labor force. Or at least they will find themselves unable to recruit adequate replacements. The Post Office in the United States was a conspicuous reminder recently. To some extent, low-wage occupations do in fact disappear: household help is the extreme case but there are many others. Some of these disappearing occupations can be replaced by cheaper substitutes, such as domestic gadgets designed to ease the burden of housekeeping. But for many jobs there are no good substitutes. Then society has to find ways of raising the wages of the occupation faster than could be motivated by any gains in productivity in the occupation itself. The prime case is the nursing profession which – fortunately – can not be mechanized to any great extent. To continue to recruit nurses, society must agree to pay them wages which are allowed to rise faster than any productivity gains in nursing. The wages must rise at least as fast as incomes increase in the country in general. When this leads to higher costs of medical insurance, this should not be a reason for higher wage demands in other occupations.

Somehow, the public has to pay the nurses. The same goes for all indispensable services in society.

What it boils down to is that the productivity gains must be shared among groups in society in a way that will maintain the necessary balance between supply and demand for all essential occupations. Economic literacy must be communicated to the union people as well as to others concerned. The unbalances and the inflation that follow upon undisciplined "grab-bag" wage demands, these adverse effects come home to the workers of the aggressive unions themselves. The same lesson should of course also be communicated to those at the high end of society's income scale. Redistributing the wealth of the super-rich will bring social profit to their own ranks. With more equality of income, life will be richer for everybody because it is safer and more human.

If the nation's income is to be shared in a balanced way, wage demands must be tempered by economic reason. This is of course easier to say than to do. It may also be easier to carry out in a small country such as Sweden, for instance. The communication of economic literacy which pervaded that country's labor wage negotiations since the late thirties and until at least a few years ago – that communication was easier to achieve in a small country. High literacy relates there to a very homogenous civilization and the economic system is easier for people to comprehend than is the case in a very large country. The counterpart of this ease of communication within a small country is of course that the distribution of income is confined to that small country. The Swedes do not share much of their wealth with other countries most of which have lower per-capita incomes than Sweden. The United States, across a whole continent, has less differences in the levels of income from one region to another than is true of Europe or even Western Europe. This country has however some sectional differences, mainly between the South and the rest of the nation. There are other problems too such as that of ethnic minorities. And finally there is the sheer geographic size of the country which makes the communication of economic literacy a daily problem. Foreign trade is also much less important to the economy of the United States than is true of any nation in Europe with the exception of the U.S.S.R. This is a consequence of the size and the many-sided development of the national economy. American workers will therefore not be as easily persuaded by export-industry arguments as is true in Sweden or England where export difficulties lead to unemployment in a way that the workers understand.

The communication of economic literacy in the United States is bogged down by all these causes from the past. But they can no longer excuse the failure to make the grabbing for income more rational and civilized. The need to have economic growth with not too much inflation calls for more enlightenment of workers – and of all who earn income. How a growing economy functions must be communicated to the people if their demands for income are to relate successfully to what the system produces. This society has the option to achieve economic maturity for its public. The option risks to be foreclosed unless there are economists who can get their message across to all kinds of people.

International sharing

International sharing is a more complicated problem. For a long time now, the rich nations have been trying to help the poor countries. Just now in the early 1970's both sides seem to be disappointed. Many people in the rich nations feel that the poor countries have not used the aid they got very well. In the poor countries, there is an increasing uneasiness about the whole thing. Many of their people doubt that the rich nations are really helping them. Coming in with large numbers of technicians and advisers looks like a new kind of colonialism. And maybe, in the complexity of international trade, the rich nations are earning more than they are spending on helping the poor countries.

There is something to be said for this. When the United States, just after World War II, helped Europe through the Marshall Plan, this country helped itself to larger export markets at the same time. Economic recovery in Europe helped economic expansion in the United States.

Basically, the same applies across the whole globe. If we can help a poor country to expand its economy faster than it would do by its own means, this will also expand the markets for our exports. The analogy with helping the poor within one's own country is quite clear. That too helps business at home. And the same principle applies to the world economy.

The foreign aid which we have given in recent years has seldom been outright gifts. Most has been loans on more or less easy terms. Lately, repayments on the loans have begun to amount to about as much money as the new loans. By no account can we say that foreign aid has been very costly to donors such as the United States, Europe, or Japan.

Most of the foreign aid, whether gifts or loans, has been used by the poor countries to buy goods in the rich nations. It should not be difficult to understand that this has meant an economic stimulus to the rich countries, just as the Marshall Plan was to the United States. Shipments for foreign aid have meant increased demands on many industries. One of the most visible cases has been the disposal of American farm surpluses.

And here is where the great misunderstanding has come in. The public learns from the newsmedia about the cost to the United States' Treasury of this foreign aid. The public believes that this treasury cost comes out of their tax money – that they are so much the poorer for it. What they do not learn is that without this foreign aid there would be less production in their country and less income – which of course means less tax revenue. They would also risk more unemployment.

It is actually an open question who profits most from foreign aid – the rich countries or the poor. But there can be no doubt at all that it is in the self-interest of the rich nations to help the poor.

Foreign aid can help to increase the movement of goods and services across the globe. It can also increase the rate of expansion for the economy of the world and all its countries. Foreign aid should be greatly increased, not cut back as now happens. Reduction of foreign aid would be followed by more trade restrictions both in the rich and the poor countries. That will only slow down the world's progress. It will also postpone the day when the underdeveloped countries may join the optional society. That delay is dangerous. The longer the poor countries have to wait, the greater the risk for political explosions and economic catastrophies that could jeopardize our own options.

Foreign aid is much more than money. Money seems to be the easiest part of it, if only people could realize what is the use of foreign aid – what is it to us and what is it to the other side? Then, people are slowly getting out of the naiveté that international communication is above all electronic media across the world. The global interdependence which the electronic media have dramatized is focused on the almost universal quest for economic development. Economic development hinges on much more than economic processes. It is also a tough confrontation with different cultures, social ideals, historical traditions, and political goals. The problem is highlighted by the "foreign accent" in international relations.

The foreign accent in international relations

The foreign accent in international relations is not only the twist in pronunciation when a stranger speaks our native language – or when we try to speak his. There is a more complicated case which the London *Economist* calls "Transenglish" – English used as a global "communication language" or Lingua Franca. Besides the twist in pronunciation, there is also a certain emphasis in the use of words and sentences. This stems from our different value systems and habits of thought which grope for their own specific expressions in a common idiom or vocabulary while creating an undercurrent of new meanings.

These cultural difficulties of foreign relations cause what many foreign-service people have called the "re-entry" problem. It is well known from our Peace Corps workers. The same is confirmed by the technical specialists and students who have got their training in one of the advanced countries, when they come home to their own emerging nation. And this is because all of them get "brainwashed" abroad. They receive not only technical training, but like the Peace Corps workers they also get penetrated by a foreign civilization and its values. This is inevitable because there are numerous links between the technology of a country and its culture, atmosphere, spirit. From a practical viewpoint: the Peace Corps worker abroad must know the values of his host country and link his teaching to their goals. At the same time he cannot get rid of his own culture which continuously rubs off on his teaching. When returning home he then finds that he has changed his own cultural outlook. The same happens to the specialist trained in an advanced foreign country for his own emerging nation. If the specialist tries to teach facts and nothing but facts when he comes home he too will soon find out that his new technology has been conceived by him in a foreign atmosphere. His home audience will feel that he is from outer space as far as their values and goals are concerned. His professional progress will be nil until he links his new technology with old accepted attitudes from the ideology at home. Only that can make his technology meaningful and practical to his own people.

There is no technical field where cultural confrontation is so dangerous as in the field of economic planning. A western-trained economist is all too likely to think in terms which may be adequate for planning in a rich country. And this may lead him to make mistakes which his own poor nation cannot afford.

In a wider sense cultural differences mean that the concept of income is ambiguous. When people do not really want the same things the world over, income differences cannot be reduced merely by sharing what we have. A deeper interpretation of economic options is necessary. These options can get international meaning only if they are communicated in a way that makes sense to national or parochial communities. The work of exploring how this communication is done has barely begun.

Communication as income

Communication is not only a means to promote economic progress. It is also part of that progress. Access to many-sided and richly diversified communication from all kinds of sources is an economic good and a very important one at that. The proof of this is that we are willing to pay money for the access to communication. There is no doubt that this willingness stands in some proportion to the quantity and quality of the flow of communication which one buys. Books, magazines, newspapers, movie tickets, radio receivers, television sets etcetera, all of them cost money. And cable television is not for free, either.

There are people, of course, who may buy a color television set just to "keep up with the Joneses." And there have been rich merchants who have bought whole libraries although they never read a book. But such cases are a thin fringe on the market for communication. The bulk of all money paid for communication sources is spent for their contents' sake. People who spend the most in this way are the most interested in the contents of their buy. For instance, advertising about performing arts and literature in the various communication media proves, by its advance publicity and by its scope and vigor, that very large economic interests are at stake both for sellers and buyers.

Since access to communication is an economic good, it is clear that our real income is larger when this access is unhampered. It also follows that censorship would make us poorer. Censorship would mean that we could not use our own money to buy the communication we want most. Such a limitation would make our money less valuable. For the same amount of income in money, we would be poorer.

This says something very important about dictatorship states, and the monopoly in communication by their ruling groups. The dictators and their retinue have arrogated to themselves a whole class of economic goods which they withhold from their people. How much poverty this can mean is evident to anyone who has tried to read newspapers such as *Pravda* and *Izvestiia*. These organs are not only deadly tedious but also repel the common readers by flagrant one-sidedness and political timing of the news. As is well known any severe rationing produces its own black market. Strong popular demand for a different kind of publicity pops up in numerous illegal publications from clandestine printing presses which keep operating at great danger in a police state. By comparison with *Pravda*, newspapers in Communist Yugoslavia appear lively and well informed. This does not mean that they are free of censorship. But the government's monopoly on communication seems to be more generous here to its people. This may have something to do with the influence of workers in the management of industry in Yugoslavia. The "gatekeepers" of the flow of news to the communication media seem therefore more responsive to the public's demands and human interest.

If dictatorships are relative, so are democracies. The freedom of speech and press is much greater in the United States than in any ever so benevolent dictatorship. There are however some limitations and they do not come so much from the government as from groups of citizens living in a parochial setting. The past has had a great deal of localized tyranny in America. Even though most of it has faded away, there may be vestiges lingering here and there. But the options are essentially open. If some news is suppressed in some papers, some competitors will bring it out in others. In the United States, the "underground" press is a booming, highly profitable business. And when some kind of communication is banned, such as cigarette ads on television for instance, we can rest assured that the ads would be back in no time if there were a strong demand for them among the general public. Just write your Congressman!

Power as income

The monopoly of communication in a dictatorship is no accident. Dictatorship, by definition, monopolizes power. And that can not be done without control of public communications. In a sense, the power to communicate equals power. But then, power, too, is an economic good. The proof of this is again that where it is at all possible, people are willing to part with some of their money to gain power or to influence the power game of society. Wealthy Americans sacrifice some of their wealth to be elected to political office. Other people throw in a few dollars and often a good deal of unpaid work as campaign contributions. The counterpart value of these sacrifices is the feeling of power – to influence important decisions or at least to be with those who do. In a democracy, the political organizations are competing with each other. No matter how old and entrenched a well-organized party may be, if it proves too little responsive to public opinion, there could be drastic changes. They risk, among other things, that a new party emerges and upsets the traditional balance. In short, political participation from grassroots and up, is among the options for which we may make economic sacrifices. But as usual, every option we use is at the cost of something else.

Here is where we must clear up the meaning of equality under dictatorship. Even when the ruling groups or parties don't get corrupted in a conventional sense – most of them do – still they are all corrupted in a different way. Power without competition is unearned psychic income which the "New Class" enjoys alone, denying this first-rate good to the citizens at large. When Lenin hijacked the Russian revolution, he created a new kind of state: the state where the enjoyment of political participation is extremely unequal.

The lack of access to political participation for most people in a dictatorship forecloses many other options for them. For instance, those in power decide what merchandise will be available on the market. Whether there will be cars, television sets, or even decent housing does not depend on people's preferences for how they want to spend their money. It is decided at the center. The economic organization of agriculture, to take another example, is decided by party ideology and strategy. These decisions are taken over the heads of the farm people without regard for the farmers' expertise on the efficient management of their own work. Another case is the disregard for industrial pollution. Technocrats in heavy industry always get their way even when they ruin an irreplaceable natural treasure such as Lake Baikal. The public may rumble but it has no effect.

Democracies come in even more diversified forms than dictatorships. Grassroots participation in the game of power is more restricted in countries where the people vote for party lists rather than for individual candidates. For instance, let us look at Sweden. The country is ruled since 1932 by a well-organized Socialist party. It has therefore had time to create a "New Class" as in Eastern Europe. Meantime, the old upper classes still live comfortably in cordial coexistence with the new. If one takes a look at the Swedish *"Who is Who"* some striking features come out from the social register. Almost everyone who is somebody either is the son or the daughter or other relative of someone who was somebody, or is or was a functionary of the ruling party or a relative of a functionary. Quite a few are at home in both classes. The new Swedish drive for "more economic equality" gets an interesting sidelight from this. The paradox of it all is that with two kinds of upper classes filling all the slots of public life there is well-nigh nothing left for a simple proletarian with no relatives or party connections.

CHAPTER V

THE POLITICAL ARENA:
OPTIONS AT HOME AND ABROAD

Some will have guessed it already: when affluence liberates from the economic bonds of penury, it should also lift some of the shackles from other workings of society. Economics in the wide sense equals politics.

In many political and social areas the options are widening. Less and less, we are bound to say: this is how it has to be. More and more, we get the option to say: this is how we want it to be. Communist literature on social development makes frequent use of an adjective meaning "inexorable" (*neuklonnyi*). This concept is obsolete. Whatever validity it may have had in those bygone days of mass penury from which the new theocracies drew their inspiration, under to-day's high-productive technology there is very little that is inexorable. The options are wide and challenging. If we choose to use the options!

The problem is magnified and its complexity compounded by the interdependence of the globe's many cultures and countries today. With everyone around the earth listening in on each other's mass media, all domestic and even parochial problems may become the world's concern. When a low-ranking biology teacher at a Midwestern university wrote a letter to a student newspaper and advocated sexual freedom, he was summarily fired. The next morning the whole globe commented upon it. But even though the world public gets the same news, the peoples are often so far apart in their cultures and in their attitudes and reactions to a piece of news that we can question whether they are really contemporary and living in the same world.

The expansion of options in the political arena will be most obvious in economic policy and organization of society. Here it can be shown that many different alternatives will serve society in about the same degree. This relaxing of limitations may carry over into other facets of society such as class divisions, women's equality, liberation of national and cultural minorities, types of schooling and education, and the various phases of "participation" – politically and otherwise.

Many options – economic and other – will remain open only on condition that the political system permits it. It is common sense that the political system should encourage the new reality of economic mass affluence and allow it to liberate from routine and conformity. Whether it will do that, depends above all on those who have a chance to be choosy: whether they actively protect and develop these possibilities or just let them slip out of their hands.

Then we must remember also the dual role of power in society: power as an instrument and as a desirable thing in itself. Does the politician wish to serve others, or is his main goal to feel powerful? The two roles are mixed up with each other, perhaps more often than not, and the mixture may or may not promote economic choice and the individual's liberty to communicate.

Power as an economic good cannot be left out here. With the unsettling effects of change accelerating the world over, the risks of a "1984" are very real. Power as an over-riding goal of a ruling monopoly party would, as Orwell saw with sharper eyes than anyone since Hobbes, also lead the party to inflict poverty intentionally on the masses. In "1984," the party makes them poor not only culturally but also materially. They even contrived to make the language poorer. Their most successful device for power and central instrument of control was the "Newspeak." That vocabulary prevented anyone from even thinking any heretic thoughts. This is how it will be under any such power concentration, whether it hails from Lenin or Marcuse, from Mao-tse-tung or Che Guevara or whoever gets a free rein for this kind of addiction.

In "1984" there was two-way television to control the population. But the flow of communication was one-way: it came only from the center. In our optional societies, as long as the pipelines remain open, the alternatives for public communication are increasing. A case in point is the so-called "public diplomacy." People nowadays are supposed to be so well briefed about public affairs that the crowd sometimes takes over the delicate negotiations with a foreign world. To see this public diplomacy in action, take a look at the demonstrations around the globe. Or suffer with the individuals who try to get their relatives freed from enemy prisons.

Alternatives of economic organization

High productivity leads to options in more ways than just in production and consumption. It also creates new options in the manner in which society is organized for economic and political and other purposes. The effects of these choices may run deep. What kind of society are we going to have – what kinds of characters are formed in the education of the young?

A classical case of expanding options is in the economic organization of agriculture. The farm problem in America and Europe is a central instance of the meeting of economics and politics. Since decades we have been exposed to the arguments for and against the family farm versus "factories in the fields." The debate generated more heat than light. Only recently has it become clear that "factories in the fields," the large-scale organization of agricultural production, does not really serve society and its consumers any better than do the family farms. The owners of such "factories in the fields" would of course have higher incomes, individually, than family farmers. But they would also be fewer and need more hired workers who would earn less than family farmers, so there would be less equality of income. The public would not get its food any cheaper. As far as consumer welfare goes, the family farm may be here to stay.

The old assumptions about the blessings of large-scale production in agriculture died hard, but now they have been demolished. It is remarkable, however, that the alternatives – the family farm versus factories in the field – are so close to being equal in productivity. And this near-equality reflects a basic productivity of known technology which is so high that any difference in the form or organization has comparatively little effect on actual productivity. This argument works both ways: the large-scale farm is not decisively superior, but neither is the family farm. If by some special analytical approach the family farm were to be shown to be actually superior to the large-scale farm, the difference would still be moderate. From now on and hence forth, in affluent countries, it does not really matter to consumers, or to society in general, how the farming industry, and its section of society, is organized. The options can be left to those directly concerned.

This conclusion would have been less obvious a few decades ago. As long as the farmers' income represented a sizeable part of consumers' spending, it did matter what kind of farms we should have. The Communist scream for "large-scale agriculture," unfounded as it was in the technical facts, did at least concern a question of some economic consequence. It could still make sense to investigate and find the answer to questions such as, would large-scale farms produce cheaper than family farms – or vice versa. A difference of a few percentage points might still have been worth going after if the difference could have been established with confidence.

This is where high productive technology changes the whole scenery. Today in America, farmers' net incomes represent merely 3-4 per cent of the national product and their gross receipts maybe 5-6 per cent of consumers' expenditures. Tomorrow, or close to year 2000, the share will be, say, 1-2 per cent of either. What does it matter, then – to consumers – whether one kind of farms produces in a way that is a small fraction cheaper than does another kind of farms? Both kinds have proven themselves competent to put into practice the big gains in productivity which advancing technology makes possible. Both kinds of farms are on essentially the same plateau of high productivity. Exit the classical "farm problem." It has been solved; not by Congress and not by default, but by technical progress, economic growth, and rising affluence. The farmers can have the farming system they want; Congress and the people do not have to tell them.

The farmers? Which ones? The family farmers who want to stay – or the corporate farm managers who want to move in and take over the land? The technocrats might just do that if they really put their minds to it and if no one else cares enough to stir up an issue. The means for such a takeover are in economic muscle – larger total resources, more flexible credit, backing by the financial resources of the same corporation or conglomerate, ultimately also tax advantages. With economic muscle, higher efficiency in serving the public is not really needed for a successful takeover.

So, whose choice is this? Are farmers the only ones interested in the issue, or does it concern other people too? If it does, they may opt for applying their political means to curtail the use of economic muscle and defend the preferences of a democratic society.

The preferences of a democratic society may for instance want to preserve some of the inherited forms of rural life with its relative equality and its individualism – as we know them in North America. But there are other societies which also have ideals to defend or establish. In Israel, a peculiar kind of collective farm known as *kibbutzim* was created to promote a new type of human personality. The kibbutzim succeeded because the settlers in these communities wanted it. In the Soviet Union, collective farms were also created to transform the mentality of the peasantry. But there, the effort became a dismal failure because the peasants did not really want the collectives. In similar ways, land reforms in emerging countries may serve or hinder the development of the economy and the people. Their success or failure will depend upon how close their social ideals are to the mind of the farmers. But the effect of social reform is never neutral. Land reform will create one kind of society, its absence will give way to another sort of community.

The farming industry was chosen as an example because of its relative simplicity. In much more complex ways, factories, offices, universities, recreation – outdoors and indoors – hobbies and all else can, more and more, be organized in one of several fashions and still make sense. How the tax system in the United States has favored the one-family dwelling – and thereby the car – should convince anyone that society has the power to draw its own profile. This is especially true when the options are mainly for convenience and emotional preference, and economic choices as conventionally defined are not really at stake.

Some exotic analogies begin to surface. European and American factories, for instance, have foremen to act as intermediaries between the engineers and the rank-and-file workers. Here and there in the literature on economic development, the factory foreman is pointed to as a key figure whose training takes more time than anyone else's in the labor hierarchy. Then out of Japan comes the stunning news that they do not use foremen in their factories. Something else is at work to make the shop function smoothly. And these Japanese factories give the rest of the world a good competitive run for their money. It is also almost axiomatic to a Westerner that industry must use promotion and pay increases as incentives to superior performance. Even the Communist countries do a good deal of this ("stakhanovism" in Russia). Then again, Japanese industry uses security and honor as incentives to obtain the same results – and how! So what is wrong with security and honor as incentives in the universities? Is a secure person necessarily less efficient than a constant risk-taker?

The trade-off between management systems may not even be the same in different cultures, or for people of different educational background. Only this much is certain: as incomes climb really high, people should be able to reach more or less the same productivity even though they are organized in quite different ways. Not just any conceivable way; there are ways which are unsuitable under any circumstances. But there are more and more options of organization, both for economic production and other vital functions of society.

A case of this modern ambivalence is in the attraction of the large city. It used to be a magnet to most people who had a chance to go there, largely because it was a much more optional place than the small town or village. The lessening of its force of attraction has something to do with the wider options to come by the same amenities elsewhere. Radio and television bring theater into the living room, rapid transportation carries luxury goods into peripheral shopping centers, and so on. But such a new trend is less compelling than the old, and downtown does not necessarily lose out altogether, as the European cities testify. Many American cities also begin to revive Main Street both through new cooperative apartment houses and by elegant shopping malls. These contrasting trends in urbanization provide a new facet of competition in an increasingly optional society.

Some "isms" in competition

Any choice between capitalism and socialism now relates to outdated concepts. It is as if we were asked to choose, for our transportation, between a horse-and-buggy and a Ford's Model T. The early automobile engineers borrowed surprisingly much from the design of the buggy, as if enchanted by the phrase "a horseless car" – a car without a horse. The special requirements of a rapid motor vehicle were only gradually explored. And no longer is the automobile's most noted characteristic that it moves without a horse.

Now the buggy is all but extinct, and the automobile has come a long way from its early designs. We have even begun to realize that the individual car is no solution to the problem of moving millions rapidly and efficiently.

Even more, classical ideas about capitalism and socialism are obsolete. Classical capitalism hardly exists any more and modern ideas on social ccntrol have come a long way since the days of Lenin and Kautsky. Classical socialism was fascinated by the nineteenth century concept of ownership as much as early car designers were of the buggy. What classical socialism tried to do was to put state ownership in the place of private ownership. In the infancy of the modern industrial state – not very many decades before it came to maturity – even the sharpest and most dispassionate thinkers were not able to visualize what the future would be like. The revision of Soviet socialism has led their leaders to pick up one concept after another out of the toolbox of free-enterprise economics. It is a slow and clumsy process, by no means as smooth as the technical adjustments of the automotive industry. In this process, the essential concepts of classical socialism are refuted; it takes place behind a smokescreen of ideological Leninism, but the concepts are refuted just the same.

Industrial affluence gives so many options for actions that the ideological smokescreen is needed. The essential power structures must be protected when various political cultures confront each other in public dialogs around the world. Increasing use of modern communication media has sharpened the competition for the public mind which is more well educated in technology and more interested in economics than ever. The different political movements close in on each other on a scale never experienced before. On the surface in this global debate, the different political cultures – Communism, Socialism, Fascism, Catholic-inspired Christian Democracy, or just plain Liberalism and Conservatism – are getting more and more concerned with demands for economic and social reforms. All of them pay less attention to their own political egos, Party or Church authority. Their opposition is more and more looked upon as problems possible to solve. In fact, their communication is often so colorless in their public dialog that it is difficult to draw a sharp line between their political profiles. Colorful vocabularies specific to one ideology or the other have often disappeared or are toned down, the Latin of the Church is translated into the common man's language whatever that happens to be. Economic and technical terms crowd the messages from the different political civilizations. To their publics, the ideology, or God, is dead and the spirit is confused with the technical transmitter of the message.

All this is in sharp contrast to the earlier public communication from the various political and ideological quarters. Before the coming of the affluent society, labor relations and other economic issues had been treated with a few exceptions in a conspicuous framework of power policy by the different ideologies. Moscow or Rome, and their affiliates around the world, stressed in their public dialog their concern for their own power and influence. The social demands they made were few. If any attention was paid to the opposition it was because of its strength or weakness. And under any circumstances the opposition was always described in a colorful vocabulary as the root of all evil. The social program turned into a demand for more power for the ideology and its glorification. The social problems could be solved only according to the doctrine or the faith.

But it is not this authoritarian model of communication that came to dominate the new patterns of public dialog in the affluent society. It was rather the model of communication in France, England and Scandinavia which came to shape the new profiles in international conversation. Mr. Khrushchev and Pope John XXIII became the symbols for this new style – or so it was believed. The Kremlin and the Vatican toned down their colorful idioms. Party jargons and Church Latin yielded to concepts for technology and economics, and to national languages. The demands for social reforms increased at the expense of the references to Party or Church. The opposition lost its all-black image and the Devil became a practical problem in technology or economics. On the surface, there was a new confidence and optimism. This new balance in communication could be seen in many different political cultures in places as diverse as the American Rockefeller Panel Report on Prospect for America (1961), Khrushchev's New Soviet Communist Party Program and John XXIII's famous encyclical New Light on Social Problems. The new balance in style was followed up in Pope Paul VI's controversial message on birth control in 1969. And President Lyndon Johnson went farther than anyone in the new democratic style in his speech "To Shape a New Political Environment" (1966).

The new profiles in communication – more attention to demands and practical problems than to one's own ideological ego – easily swayed the public. Many came to believe that something essential had changed in the attitude of the political movements. The time seemed to have come for reconciliation, coexistence or ecumenic cooperation. However, if one analyzes the undercurrents in the new democratic style, a more familiar pattern comes to sight. The old authoritarian centers in Moscow or Rome use the new balance in their communication to build themes that are so frequent that the deepest interest of the politicians still concerns their own Party or Church authority. The ideology's seal is strongly pressed on any social issue up for reform. This ideological sealing attempts to justify the vested interests of the old authoritarian power structures whose original rationale is vanishing among today's expanding options.

What we have now – in most parts of the world, in fact – is a spectrum of social systems with varying degrees of social control and varying degrees of centralization versus decentralization. The rearguards of laissez-faire economics are debating the merits of fiscal versus monetary controls on the economy. Both of these are instruments of control so central that they might render unnecessary much direct interference in the affairs of private firms. But controls they are, just the same; not "laissez-faire."

Matching this are the new tendencies toward decentralization, where central controls have already been achieved. All the "new systems" in Communist countries are groping for less central control and more making of decisions by people on the spot. That might make a socialized plant difficult to distinguish from a private firm. The most obvious merit of the private property system is of course the ease and directness with which detailed decisions can be made.

Symptomatic of the need for decentralization are the para-public corporations which here and there have begun to offer an alternative to direct bureaucratic public administration. The Indian Statistical Institute, the Rand Corporation, and several European organizations carry out work which used to be done in central bureaucracies, but now achieve it with less red tape and at less cost. The just established United States Postal Corporation is no isolated sign of the times.

Classical socialism has become obsolete because the classical concept of property is out of date. Socialism turned against the nineteenth century property relations and wanted to "socialize" these. But nowadays it is hard to see what there is to socialize that is not already working *as if* it belonged to the public powers. At the same time we now know that public powers may socialize just anything they want and still may find that a good deal of it actually escapes their effective control. In many ways these industries must be run in much the same way under public as under private ownership. The conspicuous example of this is the British steel industry and its socialization. Sometimes even central bureaucracies contain small quasi-private domains which presidents and cabinet members seem unable to control.

So, now we can choose, not between two mutually exclusive principles of private or public management of the economy. Socialism and laissez-faire in their dogmatic purity are both equally sterile. Instead we are faced with options which include an infinite variety of combinations of public and private rights to make decisions. The question is not, shall we have social control but rather how much control, where, when, how, and by whom? The problem is not whether we shall have autonomy of firms and other places of work and business, but how strong should their autonomy be? How much institutional protection is necessary, and how much risk taking should be permitted?

The modern principle of expanding options penetrates the whole arena of public affairs. Here, as in the market place, the trend is on the increase.

To show the absurdity of extreme solutions to complex problems is easy; the difficult thing is to tell apart the options that are only a little different. As a case in point, we just discussed the future organization of American agriculture. But any number of parallel topics and choices could be brought up and dramatized. In Europe, for instance, co-operative stores make an excellent contribution to competitive business as long as they remain rivals with other stores in the same markets. But whenever the co-op is the only store within miles, it turns as unimaginative as any private monopoly. Those who have experienced this rivalry want it to continue. They do not want either private or cooperative business to prevail, they find their competition profitable to customers. This will also preserve the most options. So, whose choice is it? Apparently the choice belongs to a public which has the option to patronize both kinds of stores and thus keep both alive.

The relativization of property in modern time takes on many forms. Above all it is practically impossible for any private tycoon to do "what he pleases" with large wealth. Most of the assets are real estate and other durable investments, and most of them can exist only in the social form in which they are used. Industry is organized to serve the public and therefore goes a long way to function as if it were socialized. Extreme and dramatic are the cases of the pension funds of large corporations, as we have mentioned earlier. No one can dispose of them, so who owns them really? One can perhaps dispute whether such a "para-proprietal society" based on private corporations really is a fortunate social arrangement. Here, as before, we may argue that these pension funds, like the Mediaeval "grand domain," tend to make bondsmen out of their beneficiaries. Social security across the board of a whole country permits more mobility and therefore more options.

The balance of order and freedom

The conflict between safety and freedom has any number of bewildering facets. To maintain one freedom often requires another regulation. And those who have job security may be free to take risks which they could not afford if they were independent as birds under the sky. Between the extremes of anarchy and rigid despotism, an intricate balance must be kept if practical freedom is to be maximized. The simplest illustration is that of the traffic rules. They prohibit many things which some individuals would like to do. But just because of this the rules bring a maximum of options to the entire motoring public. The individuals who would like to flout the rules now and then also benefit from the public's general compliance with the rules. Zoning is another example where the prohibition of some actions by some individuals makes life better for everyone, including those who must be reminded of their duties.

Pollution control, garbage disposal and law enforcement all rest on uniform coercion. None of them can only rely on the goodness of the human heart. The slum dwellers who throw garbage out of the window make life miserable for their neighbors and for themselves too. The chain smoker in the airplane pollutes his own air as well as his fellow passengers' bronchi. And the police protects the peace of the mafia captains and their henchmen too. Even the most successful criminal would in fact lead a better life if the police system had been efficient enough to prevent him already from starting his career.

Without organized sanitation, the affluent society's garbage heaps would be all over the place. And without police there would soon be such anarchy and breakdown in food production and distribution that there would be nothing to eat even for the criminals. This is not just fiction. During World War II, Denmark's entire police force was imprisoned in German concentration camps. The country remained without police for 18 months. One of the world's most peaceful and law-abiding nations was steadily sliding closer to complete anarchy.

Environment control gives many examples where enforcement must touch all or none. Billboards along the highways cannot be withdrawn voluntarily. Those merchants who might do so, would be hurt in the competition with less civic minded individuals. But most of them would be happy to have a general ban on highway advertisement. That would make it cheaper for them all. When a river is polluted by the waste from industries and municipalities, it does not help either that some of the polluters would withdraw voluntarily. The remaining incorrigibles would do as much damage as the whole crowd.

So it is with the whole law-and-order issue. For freedom to function, rules must be obeyed.

An old Republican slogan said that the government governs the best which governs the least. This Hobbesian reflection overlooks what government is for. It has also a curious resemblance with the neo-anarchism of our oh so inexperienced young revolutionaries. An economist might want to reconstruct the phrase, however: the government governs best which achieves its goals with the least amount of governing that will achieve these goals. This is the general least-cost principle. In a rational society it applies to government as to all else. But to achieve reasonable political and social goals may well require a great deal of governing. Nothing proves the neo-anarchists wrong as much as the problems of environment control. Control of pollution etcetera will indeed require intensive administration.

But the least-cost principle still stands. And to maintain it, it will be necessary to control those who seek power for the sake of power. Central despoties are known, among other things, for their disregard of the least-cost principle. They often neglect it even in economic production, but their contempt for it is most obvious in politics.

The power instinct

The power instinct is not the sole province of politicians. It is a common human trait. Some social scientists appear to feel that they have a mission to control the general public, forecast their behavior, and design models for our future. In truth, nobody has empowered these scholars to program the voters. The maintenance of free institutions assumes more confidence in the common sense and sound political instincts of the man in the street. Then there is always the unexpected which may upset the delicate design of the future. The social model of behavior seldom forecasts the unusual personalities who shape history or the murder which sometimes interrupts their life's work.

Orwell's "1984" is not a prediction of what will happen in any particular year of the future. It is an in-depth analysis of how power functions in a society when it is monopolized. In the kind of one-party system which Lenin invented, it is not enough to say that all power belongs to the Party. There is more to it than that. When the party in power recruits its members exclusively among those who will find themselves at home in an authoritarian hierarchy, such a ruling party becomes a focus for all those in a country in whom the power instinct is stronger than normal. The typical *apparatchik* is a man or a woman who is strong-willed, intellectually mediocre, and emotionally cold. A large fraction of the Party leadership has received intensive ideological schooling in special centers such as the Lenin Academy. In a free society with competing political parties, the people who might become *apparatchiki* remain dispersed among other individuals in and out of politics. Only in a one-party state can the power maniacs find a single focus around which they can rally. Once they are organized, trained, and settled in power, nothing but nothing can unseat them. This succeeds essentially because such people are not interested in ideas or ideals. They are only interested in power and will do whatever is needed to hold it and get the most out of the situation. "1984" is neither a forecast nor an unrealistic fantasy. Its dehumanized police state is the logical consequence of what Lenin created. Unfortunately, it might also be the result if those who resist one-party dictatorship learn the methods of their adversaries and become too well organized for the struggle. The point was made in Europe after the end of World War II. Exuberant and suddenly zealous anti-Nazis in neutral countries and elsewhere had to be reminded by those who had experienced Nazi dictatorship from within that we may all have a Hitler inside ourselves. Nazism was not only something that happened in Germany in those years. It is something that could occur in any country that trades its freedom for law and order. That again could happen if freedom is allowed to decay into anarchy and the cry to save the law and the order becomes louder than anything else. It is no secret of course that both Mussolini and Hitler drew a good deal of their inspiration from Lenin's political techniques. The old proverb holds true also here: we turn into what we hate, not only into what we love. Our adversaries' techniques of communication are contagious in our confrontation of minds. When you fight a despot watch out that you don't turn into one.

The parallels are not far away in to-day's youth movements. Affluent revolutionaries and demonstrators cheering Mao-tse-tung and Che Guevara as heroes do not cheer for peace but for power. It is characteristic that many of those who demonstrate in America for foreign dictators are children of affluent "Establishment" families. Seldom used to work for what money can get they turn to power as something more exciting to enjoy. There is an undemocratic trend in this. When money begins to be shared by the many, it ceases to be the hallmark of an élite. Then the sons and daughters of the former élite discover that family wealth no longer makes them an aristocracy. So they turn their backs on their parents' class and ideals which have come too close to the men in the street. Instead they try to become a new kind of élite by championing causes which promise them power – real or imaginary – "power to us." Their outlet in window-smashing student riots is a cultural throwback: like the cowboys coming to Wichita shooting up the town.

Needless to say, this is not the stuff out of which revolutions are made. The affluent society can afford a certain amount of revolutionary rhetoric – in fact, many kinds of it at the same time – it belongs to that society's many options. But the affluent society is too optional to form the disciplined single-minded revolutionary cadres which only penury and hardship seem to breed.

Public diplomacy

It is the fashion today to talk about the global village, or at least the Atlantic Community. Behind this talk looms a philosophy of togetherness: we are all alike, we have so much in common – not only the globe but also its problems. The man on the global street is not a stranger, he is our twin brother and more or less our identical ego. If only we communicate with each other, all will be love and understanding.

This way of looking at our world confuses means with ends. There are more than enough of electronic media to link us together. They will bring any amount of messages to any corner of the earth in a matter of seconds. But the world is no closed parochial community. Once upon a time there existed a certain identity of minds among people around the village pump. But we do not find that kind of identity anywhere in today's complex and rapidly changing world. Instead of parochial consensus we have a chorus of competing voices trying to negotiate understanding but winding up influencing each other: politicians bargaining with people, people talking back to their politicians, politicians outsmarting each other, people taking to the streets or cabling and sending letters. All of this happens with doors and windows wide open and the voices from abroad come through loud and clear and mix with the domestic quarrel. Suddenly the Germans have strong feelings on who should become mayor of New York, and American politicians lecture the Swedes on the evils of sex and socialism. The global theater is a play without a script, the performance is continuous, upstaging is part of the act, and drama, tragedy and comedy mix with each other without intermissions.

On this theater, words are cheap, concepts are up for grabs since the audience is seldom trained or interested enough to take a careful look at the use of their values. Not even listening or looking is always encouraged, at least not as an organized effort since repetition of values is the dominant feature of this affluent world of communication. And it is the character of this repetition that colors the events and in the long run is shaping public opinion. It is also this more or less sophisticated repetition that gives the bias to the events. Despite all these shortcomings, the play of the stage is often respectfully referred to as *public diplomacy*. The public is briefed on the policy of the day by a constant flow of news from home and abroad. People have the options not only of choosing among the different newsmedia and forms of modern communication, but they can also react according to their opinion of the news.

It is hard to believe that this global cacophony could be eased by even more increasing the torrent of communication. More talk does not necessarily lead to understanding, rather it invites conflict and confrontation.

In the jungles of New Guinea, the neolithic clans negotiate their differences of opinion by talking "until the talk has become one." In organized societies, consensus of opinion all too often leads to despotism. At the biggest conclave of them all, the political assemblies at United Nations' Headquarters in New York, there is no risk of consensus. The talk never "becomes one," and it never ends either. But it is not a total waste as long as words serve as a pretext for postponing violent actions. This international dialog can not be expected to lead to consensus either. Its participants come not only from different nations but they have also different cultures stemming from different historical epochs and they have different political goals. This comes out in their use of universal concepts, such as "aggressor," "peace," "freedom," "democracy" and "land reform," ideas which are twisted according to the meaning the concepts have in the various cultures. It is this cultural twist – the foreign accent in international relations – that creates the undercurrents in communication and misunderstanding in negotiations. The same thing happens on the domestic scene when different ethnic groups or interests negotiate or just communicate. Since our news media serve the commercial market place too, the different undercurrents in our communication are a growing daily concern for any advertising across national borders.

In the global dialog these undercurrents have one useful purpose. They prevent a uniform world opinion and therefore the emergence of a universal government, both of them potentially dangerous as a rigged opinion or an authoritarian administration. But, on the other hand, the undercurrents also make more difficult the creation of a code of unified meaning for the concepts we use when we carry on our international communication.

There is yet another explanation for that. The more political leaders take part in international dialogs, the more they have to look for security and stability from their own nation and policy. They are not only searching for the limits of their country's identity – for instance, shall the United States be or not be the police of the world? But they also want to keep the identity the country has – for instance, peace and prosperity at home. The political leaders of the different nations therefore have to use double-talk in their creative performance and public diplomacy – an activity that has been studied very little. No matter how international a politician seems on the surface when he appears on Telstar or gives an interview at home or abroad, he would benefit if he were a Shakespeare. He must talk at least to two audiences at the same time, if not more. The more he masters the art of saying two things by the same concept, or the same thing by many concepts, the more wide and divided publics he will get. And the more options he creates for diversified opinions and actions or for ideas or merchandise he wants to sell. It does not matter if we call him a politician or an advertiser or only a seller on the global markets.

How destructive a consensus can be is easily seen from endless committee reports and other institutionally written literature. Once upon a time, one hundred American scholars came together under the aegis of one large endowed foundation to join their manifold expertise. They were supposed to write some constructive prospects for America. The result was a disaster. The collective wisdom of the one hundred had less to say than any individual among them. "The talk had become one," and as a glorified press release, it became just Propaganda for America when none was intended. All the high-powered expertise was smothered by symbols of a consensus of patriotism.

And so it is with most of the efforts to coordinate intellectual endeavor. The history of science shows that the creative intellect works best without explicit direction. Research that seems to be without coordination grows as if there were a plan for its development. But under the guidance of directors for research programs and coordinating committees the originality of intellectual exploration declines.

This seems to be a paradox. But let us look at the analogy of swarming bees en route to a new destination. As individuals, bees are not very bright, but the swarm seems to be brighter than any individual bee. By freely communicating between themselves, the bees together function as if they were a brain of larger capacity than anyone among them has individually. But this accumulative effort of elementary intelligence requires just the opposite of an *organized* team effort. The swarm is unorganized. All the bees communicate with all the other bees, like the cells in the brain through the brainwaves. The organized team, by contrast, resembles a platoon of infantrymen. It is as stupid as its sergeant, or worse. But intelligent scholars across the world need no directors. Like the bees in the swarm, they communicate universally, picking up the signals of communication which are the most constructive. They produce a magnificently organized intellectual effort without the help of directors and coordinators.

If we want to look at the moral of all this for a moment, we conclude that intellectual education for citizenship in a free country, and even for world citizenship, is giving the individual the communicative ability of the bee and the scientist. The citizen with an open mind will no longer be a mere spectator on the global theater or passively listen to the voice of a master at home or abroad. Listening and responding to the national and global cacophony, he is not just exposed to the "massage of the media." Rather he will use his options and carefully pick up, if unconsciously, the signals of communication that make him a free member of a free community.

Package deals, propaganda, and loss of options
The power instinct can play havoc with a great many things in the com-

munication of legitimate politics. The will to build a strong power base for one major reform easily leads to including too many issues in the same propaganda package. The necessary emotional appeals get strengthened at this stage of communication by intensive and frequent use of the community's moral values. When the reform movement finally gets into power, this often leads to legislation referring more to moral values than to the specific social problem itself. This legislation to regulate morals can not be enforced and therefore it backfires or creates a backlash.

For instance, since half a century women in the United States have been waiting for a constitutional amendment that declares them human beings to the same extent as men. It would seem that this is not asking for much. But when the nearly all-male Congress finds so many excuses for not finishing this rather uncomplicated task – in fact, no more complicated than raising the Congress' own salaries – the secular delay becomes a symbol of the subtle oppression half of mankind is up against. Besides job discrimination, this subtle pressure has many symptomatic expressions. Some of them are even so commonplace that they are not always noted. Only recently was it pointed out – by the President's Adviser for Consumer Affairs – that people in the advertisement business talk down to the majority of their customers, the housewives, as if they were third-grade schoolchildren. These ad-men must have learnt their trade somewhere, in some University, some College of Communication or Department of Advertising. They reflect a spirit of teaching where it is taken for granted that women as customers and professionals should be treated as inferior minds and second-rate human beings. Then, there are the habitual jokes about women which recall the crude jests about black people before the civil rights movement gained momentum. The disappearance of jokes about blacks is an index of the success of the civil rights movement for the black male. The persistence of sarcasm at the expense of women shows what a long way women are from full civil rights and what a task that lies ahead for their human liberation. Human liberation because if you free a slave you free her masters too.

The consequence is that when a liberation movement gets going, there are so many justified social demands to make that the issues crowd in the program for reforms. But the larger public the reformers appeal to, the fewer issues can be communicated at a time. People's attention span is in inverse proportion to the size of the audience. And this audience grows more diversified in interests and knowledge the larger it is. Then there are always the extremists who link their demands for reforms with foreign political systems – a sure way to hurt their own case at home. When

Castro is taken into the package because he offers rent free housing to the people, cadres of Women's Liberation risk to play into the hands of reactionaries at home who want to foreclose central options of women's liberation.

Some time ago, Pope Paul VI made a trip to the Far East. In the Philippines, he paid a visit to one of the poorest slums of Manila. Only the blindly faithful may agree when he told the slum dwellers what they could expect from the future: "The great illusion of our time is to think that the supreme aim in life consists in struggling for and winning economic and social, temporal and external goods. You were created for a higher good, for a Kingdom of Heaven." This transcendent purpose in life was used to foreclose all hope of options for decent livelihood. No reply from the poor was placed on record.

The same silence reigns when unwanted children's fate is an issue in connection with abortion laws. Not only are most women silenced on the subject. But there is almost never a voice from the many unwanted and unloved themselves. In some communities, many of them have been conditioned to be ashamed to be identified as unwanted. And in most societies, they seem to lack the education or influence that could make their voice heard and respected. Does the mere option for birth give them a share in society's normal options?

Other attempts to legislate private morality have backfired as we mentioned earlier. The prohibitions of alcohol, gambling and drugs are destructive enough as a breeding ground for organized crime. The ultimate in social tragedy would follow if the prohibitions really were efficiently policed. Not long ago, a widely publicized politician vowed that if elected President he would hire so many new policemen until law and order got enforced – even if it took a policeman every tenth yard along the streets of a metropolitan city. Such a vision by a one-track mind reveals the extent of the disaster that would go with the enforcement of the prohibitions. A police force of that size could not be recruited and least of all in crime ridden society. Nor could it be paid decent salaries. It would quickly be infiltrated by the very elements it is supposed to keep at bay. An accomplished police state would be a mafia state. It is characteristic that attempts at enforcing the legal ban on marijuana have brought the infamous no-knock provision which allows the police to kick in one's door without warning. The attempt to legislate morality destroys privacy and snuffs out a large part of the options we all are working so hard for.

Another case of too many demands in the same package is in the more radical attempts at reforming the election system in the United States. The two-party system functions as a great stabilizer. But the question is whether it can do that when democracy becomes entirely direct. In the traditional convention system, the parties have acted in their own interest when offering presidential candidates with potential appeal to the majority. And the majority in normal times includes the middle-of-the-road public.

"Direct" primaries will nominate several candidates, all of them well advertised "stars" backed by a great deal of advance publicity. In such a primary the extremists, the demagogues, and the man with charisma will get more of the fragmented vote than any of several less impressive, middle-of-the-road candidates. If the nomination for the final election is based on who won most primaries, the people risks very much to have to choose between two extremists of the left and of the right. Neither of them may even come close to the confidence of the country at large.

The power brokers of "old politics" did in fact quite a good job of selecting presidential candidates whom a majority might accept. This is because as "organization men" they were concerned with winning. The winner might even be a "dark horse." It was not necessary that he must be a political star to begin with, which would be indispensable under direct primaries. The deflating of the star system which we have observed to be under way even in politics could very well be reversed by a system of direct preferential primaries.

The problem here is that power is not as divisible as so many other things that people are coveting. Since there can be only one President at a time, voters might in fact be given less options when they are invited to choose directly from a roster of eye-catching public figures.

CHAPTER VI

THE URGE TO CONFORM

The community feeling which tells the individual to "do as we do" is a basic dilemma of the human condition. The expanding options of the modern world pull out some of the props which in the past have helped enforcing rather high levels of conformity in each society. The result of this, the slackening of pressure, is often resented as chaotic. Penury made conformity easier to enforce, and in a way easier for people to accept, because of its material logic. With more affluence and choices, the reasons for conformity must be brought out in the open and questioned.

Communication and social conformity

To a large extent the problem is one of communication and of ability to communicate. To be a part of a community is to talk to it or at least listen to it. To be independent means not to talk unless you want to and not always to respond when you are supposed to. In all communication there is a continuous dilemma between the too-familiar and the too-unknown. If we were all saying the same things, we would not be worth listening to. If we all talked about different subjects, no one would have the background to follow what anyone else is saying. Social contact is worth experiencing because of the combination of the familiar and the unknown. This cements us together into a community and makes our conversation mutually interesting at the same time. A basic teaching device has always been to start with the already known as a link to the unknown.

In this balance between what we know and what we don't know already the nature of communication tends to give the well-known the upper hand and therefore favors conformity. This is how it works. Everybody tries to communicate. So, they start to talk about what they have in common. This is natural, since what we don't have in common we can not express in our communication. The new fact we talk about must in one way or another be linked to our old experience. Therefore, at our first contact with a stranger we disregard the differences we believe that we know of and reach out for what is felt as our common interest. Or in other words, when we communicate we identify with things that are known to us. The unknown we don't always see even though it exists. That is why we get so terribly interested in the weather when we begin our contact with a stranger. As a rule, the unknown we can hope to master only gradually – or never! To the overconfident among us our less than 20-20 vision of the unknown may even make us believe that our view of the stranger is perfectly clear. That is why a next-door neighbor sometimes seems more difficult to understand than any stranger. We may know our neighbor well enough to realize that we do not understand him.

The interest in communication and social conformity has come to new life because of economic affluence and efficient media. In past times of mass penury, a great deal of community cohesion was necessary because of the many dangers that came from poverty. When society as a whole is poor most alternatives are no viable options. Most changes would bring the risk of disaster or even final destruction. At the village pump the law was laid down with very little latitude for dissent. A closely-knit, highly conformist community was an insurance against the unpredictable threats of the outside world. For the individual in such a society, conformity may have felt reassuring. It is a tragic irony that this conformity also made the community all the more rigid. Therefore it became unprepared for the risks for which they were not trained by their traditions. When big, unexpected disaster struck, this kind of community would shatter beyond repair. The downfall of the pre-Columbian empires in Mexico and Peru are prime examples.

Conformity is easy to live with. So it has also human laziness going for it, the more so the more stagnant the society is. Dynamic societies are uncomfortable because of the uncertainty of what one is expected to conform to. A peculiar type of "conforming for comfort" is the cultural flight known as "going native." Someone from "civilization" joins the "primitive" of his own will. When European colonizers penetrated alien continents, "going native" was always officially denounced and despised. The motive for this attitude was not merely the so to say normal anger against the renegade or the traitor. Preferring the primitive was also an insult against the "superior" colonizing people. Because of this negative attitude on the more literate side of the conflict, someone's "going native" was forgotten more often than not. Therefore this must have happened more often than we know of. The human reason for "going native" was apparently the hope of finding greater balance and harmony in an archaic, rather static culture. Such a culture has existed for many centuries and has therefore had more time to work out its inner conflicts and come into harmony with itself. Because this society is static it also offers something clear and dependable to conform to. The same explanation may go for much of the literary exotism which has flourished at intervals since the eighteenth century's sentimental worship of nature – the "good savages" and the "noble robbers." In our time, much of this exotism is given a greater chance than ever before. But it is also put to more of a test. Afro hairdos, Indian headbands and guru dresses may look picturesque on native white Americans. But they attempt more than breaking the country's national conformity. They strive to conform with something else – but how far is the foreign culture understood? And how far is this low-cost imitation simply a negation of the parental culture which is woven into their minds?

The typical rationale for conformism in the communities in the Old World was in a curious way revived in North America. Emigrants were often non-conformists in their native countries, but the threatening chaos of the frontier subdued most of them. When the members of a community came from many different kinds of background, they simply could not afford to allow each other to live out their individual culture and character. Wages were higher in America, yes; but the new communities lost in security what they gained in income. And so the small town became all too often a local petty tyranny. Across the length and breadth of this vast country these petty powers were neutralized because they were so many. The conflicts between people of diverse backgrounds were "solved," in each community, on the surface. To solve them in depth was basically impossible. Usually the conflicts faded away when the original migrants grew old and died. But an all-too obvious residual of "ethnic" conflicts is still with us. The children and the grandchildren of the immigrants went to conformist schools and churches and tried to lose the foreign accent both in English and in their parental culture. Maybe the characteristic attitude of American social science, to concentrate on "behavior" and to overlook the human soul, comes from this very situation? The immigrants' and the transmigrants' inner man could not be reached by the Joneses on Main Street. But the newcomers' behavior could be made to conform by pressures which usually were more material than psychological. A typical case is the town gambler who was tolerated until the day he began to date a lady of one of the town's established families. Then he was severely flogged and ridden out of town. (Ernest Haycox). Sociologists talk about the "acculturation" of the immigrant but how often was it mimicry instead of spiritual community? How has this affected modern America and its current tensions?

The small town by its heavy-handed conformism cut down communication to the minimum which practical affairs made necessary. Another cause of inarticulate communication was the technically very efficient American farm settlement. To begin with, a farmer tends to be introverted. With 160 acres to cultivate, back in the nineteenth century, the farmer had little time to waste on words. And when the typical distance between farmsteads was a half-mile, what little was said between neighbors had to be terse enough to be heard some distance away. "A shouting language" is how American English has been described recently.

Of course, communication has its problems in the din of industrial production too. Typical is the television commercial which features an insurance salesman confident enough to try to talk to a construction worker over the rattle of a jackhammer. "I can't hear ya" was the worker's significant response.

It is in such a culture that silence becomes great drama and the most famous actors are those who communicate by saying next to nothing. Gary Cooper became classic by doing just that.

The industrial pressure

To commerce and industry, conformism has paid huge dividends, both in the recent past and today. Early factory industry produced best and cheapest in large series of identical articles. This principle is now beginning to be modified but is by no means out of the picture yet. Large and dependable markets not only mean more income from expanding production but also lower costs because of large scale in production. They also mean less uncertainty in the business outlook and more economic stability to support the social quiet of a conformist society. A tendency for big industry to think in terms of consumer conformism is known since long and has been ridiculed until the argument has become threadbare. One of the best shots at it is in Aldous Huxley's *Brave New World,* where society's overriding purpose is social stability along with universal happiness; therefore it is necessary to manipulate the public to assure a high degree of uniformity in consumers' demand even for the luxuries that make them happy.

In a less regulated society, people are in principle free to do with their last pennies as they please. Pressures to conform will then have to use the indirect levers of persuasion. Familiar is the case of the status symbols.

They have been extremely efficient in promoting modern industry. Many gadgets began as expensive upper-class luxuries. Later the masses might get their hands on them, partly because of cheaper modern production and partly because of people's rising affluence. Some former status symbols were even converted from luxury option to daily necessity. This is how it went with the automobile in America when it caused the cities to spread out over large areas which made the car indispensable. That is what is meant by a "lock-in mechanism."

Early industry was so much identified with the assembly-line and the standardized product that it was only slowly recognized that automation would give more and more options to make the product individually different. The rigidity and inhumanity of the old-style transmission band was often the target of attacks against the very idea of an industrial society. But when Chaplin in *Modern Times* made the argument stick and set in motion a revision of thought and techniques in factory production, he succeeded not only by wit and charm but also by timing. American industry of the nineteen-thirties had begun to take note of the new possibilities. The steam engine and the transmission band were more and more replaced by electric motors and wirings. It is a paradox that automated production should permit even greater flexibility. In the nineteen-thirties it was still waiting in the wings, but its effect might have been anticipated.

How slow the planning mind is to react to new perspectives one could see in progressive Sweden just after World War II, when socialist leaders lectured the public on the necessity of foregoing the "smorgasbord" mentality of bygone days of handicraft production. The reason given was that a rising level of living for all the people would require that a limited number of articles should be produced in large series to be so much cheaper. The Swedish social democrats are not alone in their mistake. In general, classical socialism was inspired in its thought on future society by conditions in early industry and its rigid standardization.

After all, it was as late as in the nineteen-twenties that Henry Ford is said to have joked that everyone could have the color on his car that he wanted as long as he wanted it black. At that time it may have been too early to anticipate Detroit's new deal: you may custom-order any combination of numerous optional features! Automated production will allow production of thousands and maybe millions of more or less different cars without any additional cost. Once a firm makes this kind of offer, the rest of them have to follow suit. Even a monopoly in cars would have to do it, once technology made it feasible, for otherwise many customers might shift their interest toward different goods.

Symptomatic is the appearance of "special" prices. Both on cars and on other expensive gadgets such prices are offered to individual customers so often that the normal list price seems to lose any significance. The selling of these highly modern factory products again takes on some of the features of haggling in an oldfashioned peasant market. The common trait of both markets: the merchandise is individually different each time. You don't haggle about the standardized goods on the shelves of a super-market, you only choose between the many options there.

This new situation in industry sets the stage for one of the typical conflicts of today. When conformism is no longer needed because of the way the industrial economy operates, some of the standards which used to be upheld by economic necessity are crumbling. The psychological attitudes toward conformism then become ambivalent. Should one con-form to the same material standards as the neighbors – "keep up, but don't outdo us?" Or should one conform by trying to excel in achievement under the same value pattern? Or should one just forget about it, or even show non-conformism in one way or another? Some will stop conforming in order to increase their family's security. Others will do so to indulge in their own fancies. And there are still others who will apply inverted con-formism by being as different as possible.

If the industrial reason for conformism is fading, it is far from having vanished altogether. In many commodities conformism is still powerful. The ready-to-wear industry is just one of the examples, even though fashion now overflows with options.

The lock-in systems
But in yet other ways, assembly-line production and conformism of past days may tie the hands of the present and foreclose some options. The standard case is still that of the automobile. Because car ownership tended to become nearly universal in North America, housing in the urban fringe and the suburbs more and more took the form of one-family homes – helped, it is true, by tax and credit arrangements. For quite some time, the trend fed on itself. Living in apartments was looked upon as lower-class status, just as having no car. After car ownership and taxation have established the far-flung residential areas, these in turn make owning a car necessary for most people. And this keeps on even though the car has no status value any more. Mass transit systems have difficulties making ends meet in spacious residential areas because few people would live

close to any one route. Since mass transit can not provide service, home owners get one more motive for having their own cars – often more than one to a family. This leaves the mass transit systems with still fewer customers. As a consequence, the mass transit systems restrict their service even more or go out of business altogether, unless rescued by public subsidies. Car ownership, family dwellings, and absence of mass transit are interlocking features; together they are the core of a *multiple lock-in system*. By its very nature, such a system tends to perpetuate itself even when its original reasons are no longer valid. It then forecloses some options which people otherwise would like to keep open. It is a fair assumption that the lock-in would not have gone as far but for the psychological element of conformism. It seems that part of the younger generation has become disenchanted with suburban living and its one-family houses. Some express a preference for the less isolated mode of life in apartment houses. But will they find what they say that they want? Or will they grudgingly accept the system which the previous generation created for them?

All told, the car in America is pretty much a curse in disguise.

Such a lock-in of conformism hurts not only those of society's individual members who might want to use the foreclosed options. By its rigidities it also may hurt entire minority groups and, in an indirect way, do considerable harm to the community as a whole. A dramatic case in point is the Watts area in Los Angeles, scene of the first large-scale outbreak of "race" violence in recent time (1965).

Some essential facts about Watts were not brought to the public's attention at the time. Years later, an alert reporter on special assignment came to mention them. Even so, they did not capture as much public attention at that time as they would have in the wake of the violence. One important fact for any ghetto is its transportation. For the Watts area, this had actually deteriorated not long before the riot. The cause of this was the building of one of the many freeways (inter-state highways) which lacerate metropolitan Los Angeles and make it less a city than an amorphous mass of housing areas. The freeway serves the traffic between the main portions of the giant city. It is a benefit to those who use it frequently – they are mainly middle- and upper-class people. Even so, it is in part self-defeating by the urban traffic congestion it fosters. The freeway also cuts off many local streets, something that gives people living in an area such as Watts *less* access to other parts of the city than before. Many people in Watts do not own cars, and with the coming of the freeway, local bus service was reduced. A new investment at the service of the people of the conformist majority, in this case actually harmed a less conformist minority. There was a net loss of options. Watts residents now had less access to the job market across the city than before. They also had less access to the shopping centers which might offer alternatives to the supply of prices and assortments in local shops. Small wonder if so much wrath was unleashed against those local merchants who may have exploited their local customers more ruthlessly when the freeway blocked off many of the alternatives which people had before.

The same point can be made in many other cases when a prevalent mode of service or production leads to the extinction of an alternative which still might be necessary. The Coast Line railway between Chicago and Milwaukee was financially successful until the urban freeway was built. With access to this road, many commuters deserted the railway. The railway ceased to make money but was not allowed to close down because this would have thrown the rest of the commuters on the freeway too. This would have clogged the traffic and exposed the freeway as unable to handle commuter traffic alone. The parallels are many. One is the much debated passenger railway system along the eastern seaboard of the United States – the "corridor" from Washington to New York and Boston. When these railways must now be subsidized, this means that we are at last paying an up to now masked part of the cost of the sumptuous freeway system and for the lavish use of individual cars for commuting and shopping.

Imitating the rich and the powerful
A large source of conformism is the feeling of prestige people get by imitating the rich and the powerful. Again the car is an obvious case. But there are so many others and examples can be taken from any epoch of history or even prehistory. For instance, Swedish peasant costumes have been traced from eighteenth century fashion for the nobility. In some cases the very fashion magazine has been identified from which the peasantry borrowed the designs for their Sunday best. The exact mental process which leads the masses to imitate the upper classes is difficult to trace, however. An essential element must be the feeling of vicarious sharing of glamor and power. Even in our time the popular "look-a-like" contests show what a strong urge there is to emulate the idols of the screen and the political limelight. It is striking how much of this imitation that has spread beyond national boundaries. On this international level it has happened all the time since the Bronze Age. In those days when pottery from ancient Greece was traded around all of the known world, lack of

sufficient supply of the goods led to imitations. Even more fascinating is the impact of Arab power around the Mediterranean in the Middle Ages before the Crusades. Christian knights as far north as Switzerland adopted the Arabic half-moon in their coats of arms and surrounded it with a garbled illegible version of Arabic script. And as far away as England, Arabic coins were counterfeited. The counterfeiters used perfectly good silver. But the coins' appearance of coming from the mint of the epoch's superpower made them more precious than coins which only bore the imprint of petty local monarchs in England. Even farther back in time, the famous English Stonehenge was built by an architect from the eastern Mediterranean. Also this reflects a will to imitate a more advanced culture. The large stone-mound graves of north-European Neolithic may well represent an effort of petty chieftains to feel like the powerful Pharaohs of Egypt with their Pyramids and other solid places of burial.

The same phenomenon has repeated itself over the ages, in fashions even more than in technology. Dramatic was the shift in styles of dress after the French Revolution. Even countries which fought bitterly against the revolution were at the same time nevertheless caught up in some of its ideas and styles. Napoleon's hat was victorious even in countries where his armies never entered. After World War II, the pattern of imitation switched to things American. American money, hot dogs, doughnuts and cola drinks and supermarkets became the "in-thing" everywhere. Everyone wanted his share of a success. The same one could also see in the planning for economic development in low-income countries. For many years, the immediate urge was to imitate the industries and the urbanization which are identified as the outcome of economic success in the advanced countries. Slowly and painfully did the lesson go home that to imitate the success, the emerging countries should first improve their agriculture as the developed countries had done a long time ago.

However, all imitation can not be shrugged off as a mere desire for prestige. For instance, the success of American jazz music around the world may very well reflect its ability to satisfy basic emotional needs of our time. In the depth of Siberia, American jazz music went home loud and clear among people who knew next to nothing about its country of origin.

The American suburb – at home and abroad

The American experience of the "melting pot" for the most different people from all parts of the world turned into a paradox. Too many people met too fast, and instead of starting a world community, people got isolated in homogenous restricted ghettos. And the result was that the American nation at large became one of the least cosmopolitan in the modern world. Characteristic is the attitude of the American abroad. He may be on a diplomatic mission, in business, or in foreign aid. Americans in a foreign country tend to band together, get into rather little contact with the local population, and surround themselves with American conveniences and even American food. President Kennedy was not the only one who brought his own beer, cream and cigars when travelling in Europe. In one of Europe's oldest and most sophisticated capital cities, a newspaper named *The Rome Daily American* quickly succeeds in simplifying the social and political situation to that of a small town back home. And army wives in Germany and elsewhere often returned to the United States after years abroad without having learnt the foreign country's language or much of its culture. These people were not born more stupid than others. The "just can't learn" attitude is part of their civilization.

The prototype of the American colony abroad is the American suburb or urban fringe neighborhood at home. It continues the old-style small town with its garden clubs, bridge circles, and to-day's cocktail parties. The decline of the central city and the increasing suburbanization of the middle classes have given a new lease on life to some of the most parochial tendencies in American society. As we said earlier, the concept of the neighborhood school reinforces the ghetto in American life and withholds from its growing youth some of the variety which could be the best part of this optional society.

On a world-wide scale, the parochial mentality of Americans abroad is excelled only by the Russians abroad. The two superpowers confront each other in the electronic news media they wire around the globe. The news transmitted mostly reflects the super powers and their special interests. This is a fact that is deeply resented by the smaller nations in Europe and in the Third World, which feel that their own options in communication are foreclosed. The sheer weight of the United States and Soviet communication apparatus steamrolls away much of the punier efforts of national networks.

Superpower resources in money and technology may have a certain effect on the mind of the scholar or communicator who controls it, just as driving a powerful car inflates the ego of many otherwise harmless individuals. Typical is an American social scientist who once talked to an international conference of highly sophisticated communication experts from many countries and cultures. He expanded on his own research findings and then topped it off by the generous invitation: "We want to share our knowledge with you!" He never mentioned the option that there were others who could share their knowledge with him.

This parochialism is an easily discovered feature in American culture. It is less easy to say in what direction it may be changing. Logically, one could expect attrition to weaken the parochial feature with the passage of time and with intensified international experience. On the other hand, suburbanization reinforced the parochial tendencies to some extent. The peace movement of the last few years seems in a curious way to revive traditional American isolationism.

CHAPTER VII

ADDICTION, DROP-OUTS, AND NON-INVOLVEMENT

With more options at our command, the problem of addiction comes into sharper focus than before. With less cost for the necessities of life, the option comes up also to indulge more in addictions than any habitual drunk ever did in the age of mass poverty.

An addiction is foremost a distortion of the mind. Sometimes, but far from always, it is followed by a distortion of the body, particularly the nervous system. Most addictions are discussed as if they only meant that we want more of one thing: a craving without limit, or with too wide limits anyhow. Too seldom is it pointed out that most addictions are really the opposite: the excessive craving for one thing or one kind of experience masks a lack of zest for what else life can offer.

Life is both a process and a steady state. To function properly it needs a wide variety of sub-processes which co-exist in a balanced combination. This is especially true of the human mind, whose enormous scope for sophisticated mental life can be used "to capacity" only if we do not get stuck in what is one of the main sources of addiction: boredom. Among intellectuals who excessively feed on one kind of brainwork, this is sometimes called "acedia." Some other people call it spleen.

When boredom is the cause of addiction, the addictive craving is often an attempt to escape dullness and lack of excitement. But this is not the case as often as many would believe; maybe it is not even the rule. Many addictions stem from the same source as the boredom which they are believed to replace: a lack of ability or will to use the variety, that spice of life, for which the human mind is so richly endowed. Many people's addictions are more than a simple escape hatch. They are often a flight from the strain and the moral effort to live with numerous options and also the uncertainty that goes with them.

Addictions are a concern to society for a host of reasons, but here we shall take a look at their effects on economic life and human communication. It is typical that they contribute to restricting choice in both. To the extent they are many individuals' problem, they of course become society's. The point must be discussed over again, especially in this country. Here, past attempts at coping with addictions have mainly relied on repressive means. And they have created a record of failure so dismal that they have become one of the main flaws in American society.

Addictions eliminate options and narrow down the choices to be made. That is destructive in itself, but this has not always been noticed. Up to a point, addiction has contributed to conformism and social stability. At times, alcohol was a "stabilizer" by keeping people away from more serious pursuits. Spectator sports also sponge up huge amounts of excess energy. When the young begin to withdraw from this single-minded use of leisure time, the risk for riots is on the increase. The emperors of Rome already understood that bread and circus shows for the people solved many social problems. And seen from a certain angle, organized religion has been looked upon as "opium for the masses." But whether its replacement by Marxism as "opium for intellectuals" is really progress, can be questioned.

Addictions can be conformist, compatible with people's accepted social roles, or they can result in withdrawing and anti-social attitudes. In some cases they can even be both, which may seem a paradox. This was certainly the case with alcohol in many times past. And the pot smokers seem to be withdrawing from each other, even in the same room. Apparently, each has his own hallucinations, in complete isolation.

When talking about addictions, one usually thinks of intoxicant poisons. But people may also be addicted to some of life's normal ingredients such as food or work; to peculiar habits such as gambling or speeding; to novelty for the sake of novelty, as a flight from routine; to sports and games, to power and influence; to youth and sex; to particular types of art, music or literature, all at the expense of other kinds of expression; and in general someone may become addicted to most any kind of human experience, normal or abnormal.

Physical poisons

Addictive poisons are not merely signs of human failure. They are also important symptoms of what is ailing a civilization. A connection between choice of dope and type of personality and culture is suggested here and there in perceptive literature. One of the best reflections on this is in Malraux' *La condition humaine*. There one of the characters says about a friend: alcohol is wrong for him, he is really the opium type. It may of course very well be that different personality types show up with more or less frequency in different civilizations. The use of alcohol in Europe and America may have something to do with the stiff discipline of individualism which needs to relax off and on. The more adaptive, less dynamic traditional civilization in eastern Asia may make the prevalent use of opium there just as logical. An African writer (William Conton) told of the disproportionate effect whiskey could have on his people who were not brought up with it. The Indian peasants of South America's Andean highlands have for centuries been ridden with malnutrition and back-breaking physical toil. For them, their homeland's cocaine appears as a logical escape valve from the pain and fatigue of their existence.

All this makes us wonder whether the new interest in different kinds of drugs in America and Europe points to a shift in the formation of personalities. Maybe it merely means more options also in the ways of self-destruction – actually, people seem to drink more whiskey than ever.

The quarrel today over marijuana versus alcohol usually does scant justice to some interesting problems. Alcohol is not always used as an intoxicant. As a beverage it is often chosen merely for taste. In refined cuisine, distinct brands of wine or beer are carefully combined with selected kinds of food to which they add one more spice to the variety of life.

No such civilized use can be made of marijuana, LSD, or the other so-called "mind-expanding" drugs. They are always intoxicants. There is no such thing as a mind-expanding drug. The mind is at its best when it is undrugged. Those who say that drugs "expand" their minds are merely confessing an abysmal level of spiritual poverty.

Monotony

Hitler loved Wagner's music. He played his records over and over again. He never got enough. He was a Wagner addict. But he was not alone in this special kind of addiction. The public at religious revival meetings have been heard to sing the same hymn over and over again until reaching the thirty-fourth verse. And millions of young people today indulge in playing over and over again records of music of rather elementary sort. Often it is played so loudly that any refinement of expression is drowned out. Many of the listeners get their hearing impaired to the level of a sixty-year old. But there are some benefits from this bedlam. It makes conversation surplus. It is in this way that the rebellious young of today mirror the shouting communication inherited from their hard-hat fathers and farmer grandfathers.

Loud noises that risk to make you deaf are an addiction in many other cases. The Nazi mass meetings of the 1930's indulged in endless shouting of "Sieg Heil." They drowned out the less arrogant voices of individual conscience in an addictive mass experience. More recent demonstrators shouting for Ho Chi Minh and other latterday heroes are closer than they think to predecessors of whom they don't care to know anything. Here again we see in communication that your opponent is your teacher, like it or not.

In an open society with several options, the monotony of shouting communication leads to saturation in your mind and eventually to a boomerang effect. The more sane among us get fed up at the thirty-fourth verse and may go home and sin. Safety valves like that can function as long as our society has several alternatives to a message and therefore more options. But the addict will hang on and spurn the alternatives.

This is where the communication monopoly in a dictatorship makes all the difference. When television in Communist China is all Mao-tse-tung from morning to night and hardly anything else, those who would seek other options find none. In such a community it is of course extremely difficult to maintain any mental reservation or independence of mind. But even those who would try to do so for a time will eventually be permeated with a sleeper effect of the party-line propaganda and its unending drumfire. Such a society also favors those inclined to be addicted to the monotonous. It penalizes those who have a sense for balance and variety of interests.

After such an indoctrination, it becomes all the more difficult to understand people from another civilization. It is therefore logical that those who study foreign languages in Communist China are told to "speak Chinese in foreign languages." That is, their "foreign accent" in international relations is carefully planned and kept. Their Communist concepts are dressed in ordinary English words which therefore get a new undercurrent meaning and influence a gullible public.

Even our days' mental addictions in a free and open society often mirror the sleeper effect from past ages of tyranny. Inquisition in Spain, Prussian military drill and despotism of the Tsars in Russia have all left their legacies in our time.

There is a special case which we may call the reading fad or addiction to a standard story. In this age of television it has specially strong influence because many people spend more time in front of their television set than at work. But the addiction to the same story repeated over again with some variation – Perry Mason, for instance – goes far back in time.

Let us begin with Cervantes' Don Quijote, the famous wandering knight who fought windmills to protect widows and orphans. This master-piece from early 17th century Spain was written to put an end to a long-lived literary fad. And it did, by making the genre ridiculous. The *chevalier errant* (wandering do-gooder) had been treated in endless num-bers of cheap Spanish novels which no one cares to read any more.

Despite Cervantes' success, the motive about the wandering knight has arisen with surprising vitality today. Under a variety of names, it has shown up in any number of modern American television series. Most of the series were soon forgotten, but the plot lives on. "Rawhide" had a story about cattle drovers in Texas and Missouri, but they spent most of their time righting wrongs and rescuing the oppressed along the trail to Sedalia. "Have gun, will travel" was a soldier of fortune but he always succeeded at getting sidetracked into good deeds. "Route 66" makes he-roes of two car bums. They always slug the bad guys and help the in-nocent and get away with it. "Run for your life" had the ideal set-up for a *chevalier errant*. Death waits at the end of the road, the hero's own life has no value, money is no problem, so there are no ulterior motives to stain the knight's shining armor.

The motive has an addictive appeal of escapism. With social workers like that who needs to exercise our own options? Cervantes succeeded in making the chivalry novels obsolete. But what little attempts there have been to satirize American television fads have had remarkably small ef-fects. Dropping out by boredom seems to be the public's principal option.

There is also a youth syndrome that hits the eye in American television programs but most of all in the commercials. The "look-alike-mother-and-daughter team" makes no bones about it. A mature person's human worth is in direct proportion to "exercise, plenty of rest, the right kind of food, and a pill a day." However, the frequent emphasis on sexual prowess is not specific to North American culture only. There is much more *ma-chismo* south of the border. And in Italian newspapers, movies and liter-ature, one can see today that a man risks an irreparable loss of face unless he can prove at all ages that he is the entire animal. But the youth cult in the United States is more than elsewhere a relentless denial of the values growing years may add to a personality. The options to maturity of the soul are foreclosed and the civilization is so much the poorer for it. To grow physically older and spiritually more mature in such a culture be-comes a tough challenge against the bland conformism of the youth cult.

Drop-outs

The idea is as old as Antiquity. At the time of Alexander the Great, a celebrated philosopher, Diogenes, said a thinking man would need no more comfort than a dog. He lived accordingly, using an old tub for shelter. From that presumed dogstandard of disdain for material comfort the school of Diogenes was named *cynical* (from *kyne*, the Greek word for dog.) A cynic he may not have been, but his idea was not very constructive either.

At all times there have been those who got fed up with the trappings of worldly wealth. From Gautama Buddha to Francis of Assisi, they have usually turned to monasticism and withdrawn from regular society either into primitive solitude or into organized counter-society. The drop-outs of our days have any number of predecessors. Their feeling of alienation and disillusionment has echoed through the empty halls of idle affluence ever since the time of the Ecclesiastes: "Vanity of vanities; all is vanity."

At all previous ages the option to drop out has been a luxury for the few. The masses who sweated together the riches of which some privileged people were blasé, these masses had rarely a leeway to feel whether they might have been fed up with the culture of their time. There was an occasional riot now and then, but most of the time the masses toiled on and on. In previous epochs, too, the dropping out only led to some re-ordering of priorities in consumption. Production was too scarce to be much affected by it.

Now it is different. Mass affluence makes it possible for people to drop out from almost any walk of life. Even so, it still appears to be most attractive for children of the well-to-do. It is not even necessary for the modern drop-out to live on his parents' bank account. If he is serious about renouncing bourgeois luxuries, he can earn the money for his elementary needs just by a few hours' work a week. In the affluent society, real wages are that high as a consequence of high productivity in agriculture and industry. Even the Soviet Union has a number of wandering drop-outs known as *bichi* who take short-term jobs here and there. They get scant publicity in a dictatorship whose motivations they reject by their way of life.

Some drop-outs are both courageous and constructive if they rebel against parochial conformism. It is constructive to break conventions if this creates wider use of our options. To try the new is sometimes more expensive and exacting than to use the old cheap mass goods and mass habits.

A great many people do this in a selective way when they use their own judgment and choose to drop out from one thing or another. But to reject the bulk of all that modern material culture has to offer is a different matter, with different consequences.

Whether and to what extent dropping out is courageous and creative or rather cowardly and destructive, depends not so much on what is given up as what it is given up for. Early monastic groups left "the world" to concentrate on "the spirit," and a new spiritual and material culture emerged from their seclusion in the monasteries. Some of our present drop-out groups also leave the "square" world and its self-indulgence but to concentrate on . . . another type of self-indulgence, usually of addictive type.

In their more advanced and more or less organized form, the modern drop-out groups are parasites on "square" society. The connection is simple enough: they are able to abandon "materialistic" society because it is so high-productive that it permits the drop-outs to earn a living by working only a small number of hours a week. If the hippie style of life were to become prevalent, or even adopted by a large share of a population, then the economic mechanism would break down. That would leave all of us, squares, hippies and true individualists alike, to start all over again in oldfashioned poverty. And that would require, among other things, a full work week to earn a rather mean existence.

A parasite is one who lives on someone else and does not give in exchange anything worth having – if he does, the relation is called symbiosis. The hippies undoubtedly live on square society. So do many others such as artists, writers, and university professors. These people are however supposed to produce something in exchange – their tie with industrial society is symbiotic. What the hippie colonies may be producing for the benefit of the rest of us, is as yet not clear. Maybe we should thank them for reminding us of the mortality of our material affluence. But any new disease could do that much for us.

A special kind of drop-outs are those who leave the regular political process in a free country. Anarchism is sometimes preached by serious and apparently well-intentioned thinkers. But they are not entirely innocent in fomenting the anarchist propaganda among today's youth. The far-out rebels of our time promise us that more freedom will come from their revolution. But they never mention some vital consequences of their program. Quite a lot of governing and administration will be necessary for a program to tackle social inequality and environment control. If society is to adopt extreme economic equality among its members, this will require a good deal of enforcement. And here is a problem, since there is a trade-off between freedom and enforced equality.

Flight from communication

If a problem gets too tough, some people choose to drop out even from the communication about it. "We shall not talk about it." Some "just don't care for politics" or, "never look at television" or, they have "never heard of the stuff." Then there is the busy intellectual who "never reads the local newspaper, but my wife reads it." And finally, others are selective and make deliberate choices such as not reading the sport pages to get more time for other topics.

Addiction to monotony is not unusual, but dropping out from monotony is even more common. This is a lesson that the television networks are slow to learn. Their desire to reach very large mass publics by the same program leads them to believe that the programs must be elementary. It is taken for granted that their broadcast goes to a mass public most of which is very simple-minded. There are two flaws in this reasoning. One is that the television audience is not a "mass" in the psychological sense. Each listener tunes in his set to get a look at his individual interest. This of course promises a great future to cable television. The other flaw is that the networks are badly underrating their public, not the least if they believe that they can draw a clear line between "information" and "entertainment" in their programs. It is not so simple that information is the same as newscasts and documentaries or educational films, or that entertainment is just variety shows and fiction. The fact is that you can not give information without being entertaining. And you do not entertain without giving information. Each person may be limited in his interest and as to how many options he can stand. But across a large continent, the individuals who add up to a public represent between themselves an enormous variety of interests and can use an awful lot of options. Needless to say, this sort of audience will increase, the more global the newsmedia become.

It has been said that Shakespeare would never have made it as a television writer today. That seems to be true, and is very unfortunate for the networks. The Shakespeare model is in fact tuned in to the modern public needs because Shakespeare was able to write on many different levels at the same time. Therefore he entertained many different kinds of people in the same play. And he gave a lot of information and education by entertaining people of widely different background and interests.

When interest in television programs is waning, and many people stop watching television altogether, the networks can blame their own stereotype approach. But there are other bores in public life than the networks. Why cannot Johnny read, and why cannot university students spell?

Some of it is blamed on a technique of teaching known as "look-say reading." Despite the obvious nonsense of this technique it persists by the force of vested interests. The error of look-say reading is only one part of a mechanistic approach to language. Linguists think of training other linguists and so they foreclose many of the options for which other people want proficiency in languages. *Simplicissimus*, a German satirical journal early in this century, once showed a cartoon of a German schoolteacher, his wife, and their five-year old son. "Ever since he was born," says the teacher to his wife, "I have taught our son German grammar, and still he cannot say one word." It is with language as with many other things, that they are best learned in their living human context. The abstraction of the specialist is wasted on most people. Direct acquaintance with literary masterpieces attractive to children and adolescents not only stimulates their imagination and human empathy. But it also teaches them to read faster and rubs in the spelling of their mother tongue.

The essential of it is that tedious teaching makes schools boring. And teachers such as Lolita's headmistress who dismiss much of the history of human culture as something they won't need in their lives, are just preparing their students for dropping out of civilization.

The mental ability which is not schooled or exercized will be lost or atrophied. This is easy to see in some cases where an ability was never learned at all. The Chinese emperor (late 19th century) who had never heard European music before, felt that the best part of the concert was the very first. He meant the clinking sounds when the musicians tuned their instruments. And the great idol of modern Arab music is a singer who has earned her millions by an extremely refined technique which completely escapes the untrained ears of Europeans and Americans. Long ago in Africa, an Arab slave trader was shown a pencil drawing of his own face by a European traveler. Because of his religion, the Moslem gentleman had never seen a portrait before. He turned the picture around, pointed to his beard which was upside down, and asked if that was smoke. Recognition of a human face in a drawing is something we all have to learn, it is not innate.

Educators who scrap large parts of our human culture as not practical for daily use, foreclose many future interests and options for their students. Not only dictatorships can educate away options. Single-minded education fads in democracies do it too. When restive school children are drugged to be quiet under tedious teachers, the educational failure has been concealed and placed beyond remedy.

Non-involvement

The end of freedom does not come from violence but from passivity. When Nazi Germany had capitulated, many Germans ducked the moral question of collective guilt for the atrocities by asking: "What could I have done about it?" ("Was können wir dafür?") In a complex modern society it is a difficult question when we shall get involved and not get involved. In a recent election campaign in the Deep South, some politicians took the easy way out by using an old American expression: "Let George do it."

The dilemma can be described in a very simple way if we look at our habits of consumption. Sure enough, a great many things have been done for us in advance by industrialists. They produce ready-to-wear clothes, ready-to-eat food, apartments ready to move into, some of them part furnished or even completely decorated by experts. It is easy to slip into the ready-to-use things and let someone else decide the details of our taste and comfort. But, as it should have become clear by now, it is less than ever necessary that we just sit back and accept the design made for us by centrally placed production planners. It should be possible for consumers to dictate more and more what industry should produce. Especially when we think of the increasing versatility of automated industry and the ever larger share of our income which we can use as we please. It should be possible if the options are made the most of.

The question of consumer choice comes up from a different angle when economists discuss the influence of taxation on economic life. It is clear enough that taxes will influence consumption, investment and saving. Real estate taxes will limit people's will to invest in real estate. If the real estate taxes are high they contribute to making the cities ugly and the slum housing forever more decrepit. Sales taxes influence in various ways what consumers will buy and even what producers will invest in. Income taxes also have their effects, especially if they are graduated, and the effect depends on how steeply graduated they are. One school of thought says that this influence of taxation on consumption, investment and saving is not only wrong but unnecessary. The goal is said to be "fiscal neutrality." Taxes should be thought out and organized in such a way that the distribution of consumption, investment and savings would stay the same as if there were no taxes at all. Such a policy is advocated as the ultimate in consumer democracy. It would allow the individuals as consumers to decide the course of the economy. However, it is not at all clear why consumer democracy should be better than political democracy. As consumers we are simply reacting to the economy as it is. It is not likely that our individual buying or saving would express our opinion on what a long-term master plan for the economy should be. As voters we may want to use the political process to influence the economy over a longer run than we can as consumers. Socially useful investments are often made far ahead of time. When they exceed the life span of the individual, funds for them can not always be raised from private savings. It would seem that deliberate political action in a democratic system will let us decide more about our own future than the indirect influence we can exercise as consumers on the market. The political process is also more likely to favor those very options which will keep our own options open. Consumer reaction is somewhat more likely to foreclose them by default. For instance, the use of private cars in Los Angeles has created a contourless traffic mess. The subway in San Francisco will organize the city's traffic. It could not be created little by little in response to consumers' reactions, but had to be planned centrally through the political process.

But that assumes involvement by citizens. There is much more than the traffic which will be different if we get involved rather than letting someone else do it for us. As citizens we must have a wider horizon than our own private existence may feel comfortable. The sight of a crowd in New York passively watching a murder slowly accomplished in the open street, became a reminder to many people. No one ever cared to phone the police. If any individual should give signs of getting involved, there is always the criminal's threat: "this is none of your business." But it *is* our business any time anyone else falls victim of a crime. Again the political decay of Germany in the 1930's is revealing. First, the Jews were persecuted, and the rest looked on because they were not Jews. Then the turn came to Catholics, and the Protestants stood aside, because they were not Catholics. But when the Gestapo came to Protestants, there was no one left to protect them. In any society, anyone who looks upon someone else's murder as none of his business is asking for the day when he will be the next victim.

And it may all begin in front of our television set as it once began at the village pump. The decision to be involved or to let someone else do it is a question of opinions – if we use our own or if we use the ready-to-show opinions prepared for us by someone else. Church discipline in Spain made the common Christians passively look on when heretics were burned at the stake. Prussian drill and Lutheran discipline together had prepared Germans for turning their faces when Jews and non-conformists were persecuted. In other countries too, public opinion took the easy way out. England in the nineteen-thirties simply refused to believe what their newspaper correspondents told them from the streets in Hitler's Berlin (Andrew Sharf).

But when crisis really is upon us it is often too late to start building morale. Our involvement in what we feel as right or wrong grows or withers imperceptibly with the indoctrination and propaganda we tolerate or react against. It is not so unusual that we associate propaganda and indoctrination with rabble-rousers and bomb-throwing agitators and rebels and their communication. These people are not so dangerous for our opinions because their obvious message puts us on guard in more than one respect. Effective indoctrination and propaganda is much more subtle and trivial. Some of the influences come through our schools and universities. Some from our daily newspapers and other newsmedia. Their editors' and broadcasters' attitude to authority, for instance, in small daily matters coach us with a ready-to-use opinion which suddenly comes back in our instant response to times of crisis. This manufacturing of public opinion is just as dangerous to talk about as was sex not long ago. Our inner personality is involved here. And to question our own integrity is particularly painful when it has flaws. This kind of prudery has so far prevented nearly all serious analysis of the creative propaganda process. "Models of behavior" skillfully conceal what goes on inside the human mind.

Our daily news media and schools are not the only source of inspiration for our opinions. What we read for entertainment gives us also a large part of the information – whatever it may be worth – which builds up our attitudes. Here again there is a running problem of following our own taste and interest or letting someone else choose for us.

What we choose in all facets of life is reflected in our attitudes as citizens. These attitudes are decisive for the future of the optional society. Do we stay in charge of our own options? Or will those who would like to make the choice for us master our minds – and us?

CHAPTER VIII

A BALANCE SHEET

An old Chinese interpretation of life says that life consists of trivial little misfortunes of no particular significance taken one by one; the larger patterns of society and history usually escape the individual because he feels that he cannot do anything about it anyhow. So our neighbor falls off his roof and breaks his leg, and that may fill our mind for the rest of that day. And then our newspaper and television add to the day's chronicle of incidents by telling of war, traffic accidents, crime and volcanic eruptions, airplane disasters, broken-up marriages or sweet romance in high society, topped off with a fashion show here and there. The frequency of this kind of communication fills our minds since news not only informs but also entertains us and breaks our small daily routine, while making the news media prosperous.

The flow of communication conditions us to pass over the real character of our society as less significant. The expansion of options for economic opportunity, many-sided communication and personal freedom is largely overlooked in modern debate because that is not what catches people's imagination.

We have looked at the function of options in modern time and tried to visualize what an optional society might be if it is allowed to continue. And we have also tried to look at some of the forces that might be its undoing. But we are no "futurologists," we do not try to tell what will happen, only what might.

The optional society opens up opportunities for the individuals and releases them from group pressures. It is the end of reservations, ghettos, slums and neighborhood schools. On the other hand, by its very nature the optional society denies concentration of power to any favored group.

Ever since people began to build societies of some complexity, the structure has tended to be like the anthill, with masses of toiling individuals underdeveloped in body and mind as the working ants. And at the top of this society, the privileged few were allowed to grow to full size like the queen insects.

The conversion from the aristocratic set-up of penury to the potential equality of affluence just had to be turbulent and full of strife. But the overshadowing fact is that in the optional society excellence in some individuals no longer has to be at the cost of crippling the masses. Excellence in achievement may bring forth an aristocracy of a new kind. Nature is very generous. The gift of potential excellence and aristocracy in achievement can be found in individuals of both sexes, all kinds of races and their mixtures, all nationalities and social backgrounds. The optional society first gives the opportunity for this wealth of potential talent to be developed and used. The United States seems to be the first political community that invited the masses to this smorgasbord. This unique departure could not be without its flaws. Many critics of affluent America have found it a bad place to live in, full of materialism, pollution and lack of discipline. But there is one more paradox about this. For the ills of high technology the cure is even higher technology. But no level of technology works independently of human skill, accuracy and involvement. The affluent society is where you can win the whole world and lose your soul. But the optional society offers our soul back to us because it is no longer necessary to own other people in order to enjoy the world. The individual who knows his options, is free.

To realize the whole potential of a full-fledged optional society, the nature of its promise must be understood and sized up in a realistic way. The dangers that are threatening the possibility of an optional society come as much from over-rating the prospects as from under-rating them. The threats from power concentration such as in the Orwellian nightmare of "1984" are obvious in themselves. What is less conspicuous is how lack of faith in the idea of freedom could make it easier for the power maniacs to get organized. The idea of individual freedom can not live without an education which prepares Everyman to say yes to a world full of richly varied options. He must get involved with all his brainpower and human empathy and participate in his society's institutions. Without this public education of the common man to develop all his potentials and talents, the option for everybody to excellence in achievements could easily lead to new sharp class divisions in society. Then a minority of highly developed brainpower – technocrats – could use their superiority to tightly regulate the lives of the rest.

In large parts of the world the threat to the optional society comes from the deeply ingrained habits of conformism among people still living in penury or just recently emerging from it. In the United States the difficulty is more ambivalent. On one side, Americans have so long lived with substantial freedoms that they may tend to over-rate the validity around the world of specific American freedoms. Contrasting with this is the long-standing parochialism in small towns and suburbs with their own ingrained habits of conformism. Overconfidence in the validity of the American model works in several ways. The wide-spread talk about eventual convergence of the social systems in East and West relies too much on what is seen on the surface. The organization of society is not about to become the same everywhere. But all over the world it seeks its way within a broad spectrum of possible combinations in politics, economics and other social relations. The different countries will seek their combinations according to their inherited communication realms and traditional value systems. Just because we use the same technical devices and show some analogies in certain features of social organization does not mean that we are alike. Unless we get the habit of analyzing each other's communication, this shrinking world will find individuals and nations as alien to each other as ever, only at shorter distance.

Parochial conformism, and the optional society's character, have got together in the American outlook on the world. Whether to make war or make peace, both sides of the argument in this country communicate their options as if it were up to America to decide it alone. Judging from these attitudes, to the American mind the rest of the world is a projection of the optional society at home where freedom of choice is never really questioned. The fact is, however, that most of the world is not optional societies, at least not yet. If and when they once become societies of options, it is in the very nature of this kind of community that one single power, or a group of a few powers, can not rule the options for the rest of the world.